I0741940

All We Ever Wanted
EMILY GIFFIN

Page-turning . . . Timely and thought-provoking, it's Giffin's best yet."

—People

https://amzn.to/3WNATEc

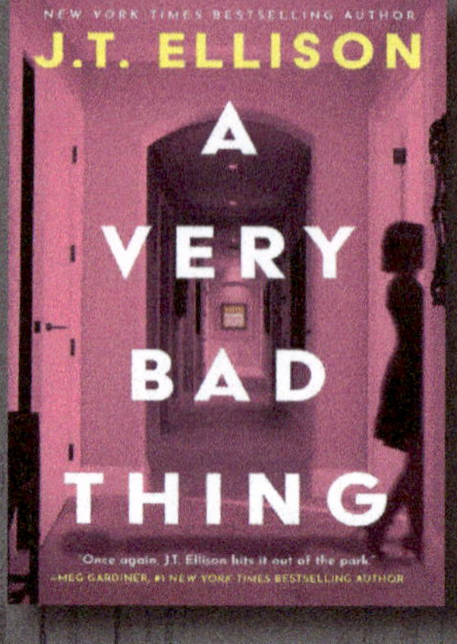

A Very Bad Thing
J.T. ELLISON

"A Very Bad Thing is a wonderfully smart, twisty psychological thriller infused with dark secrets, high drama, and edgy tension. Wow, what a ride!"

—Jayne Ann Krentz, New York Times bestselling author

https://amzn.to/4c41ktK

A Death in Cornwall
DANIEL SILVA

"Vastly entertaining with a blend of familiar characters, unrivaled plot development acumen, and artful repartee"

— J McIver

https://amzn.to/3WPoOyx

The Lions of Fifth Avenue
FIONA DAVIS

"The Lions of Fifth Avenue is a book written for booklovers."

—O, The Oprah Magazine

https://amzn.to/3LPu7al

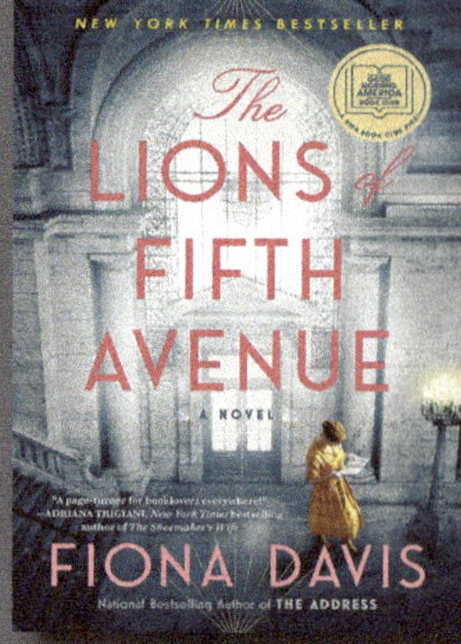

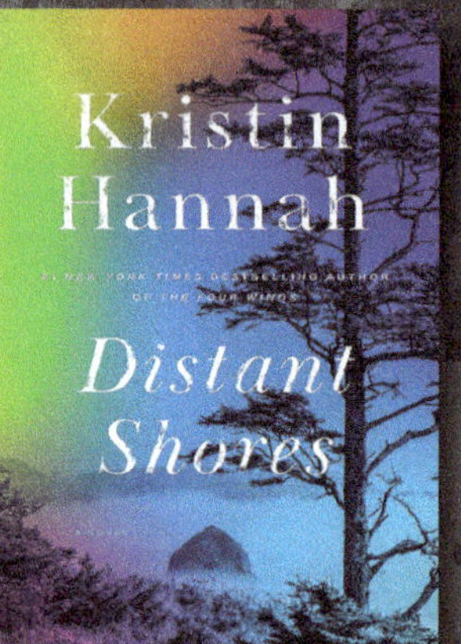

Distant Shores
KRISTIN HANNAH

"Certain to strike a chord . . . winning characterizations . . . and a few surprises."

—The Seattle Times

https://amzn.to/4d8uuco

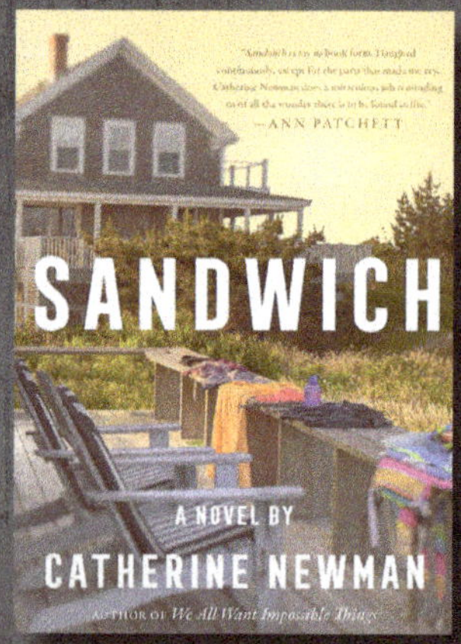

Sandwich
CATHERINE NEWMAN

"If you want a book that has you from 'hello,' this is the one."

— Ann Patchett, PBS NewsHour

https://amzn.to/3yb2shu

The Book of Lost Friends
LISA WINGATE

"A [story] of a family lost and found . . . a poignant, engrossing tale about sibling love and the toll of secrets."

—People

https://amzn.to/3WmZIoY

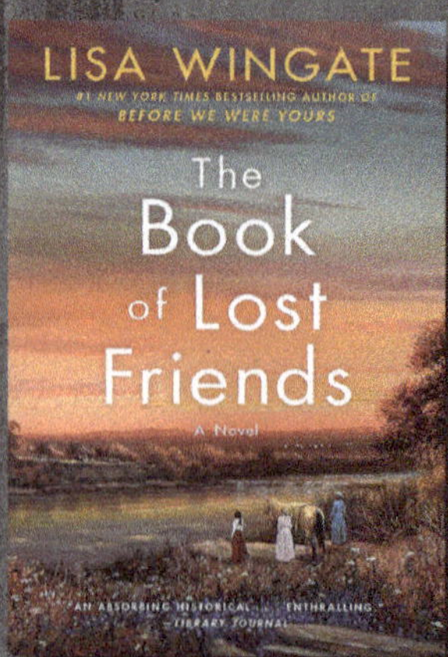

Clete
JAMES LEE BURKE

"James Lee Burke is the reigning champ of nostalgia noir."

—New York Times Book Review

https://amzn.to/3LMAImv

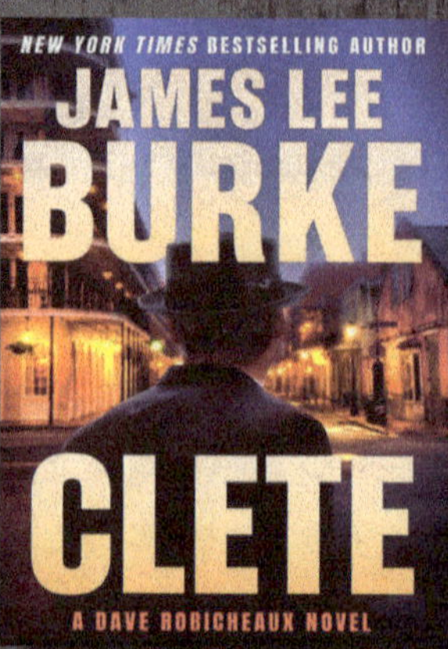

FICTION FAVORITES

Curated Novels to Enrich Your Reading Journey

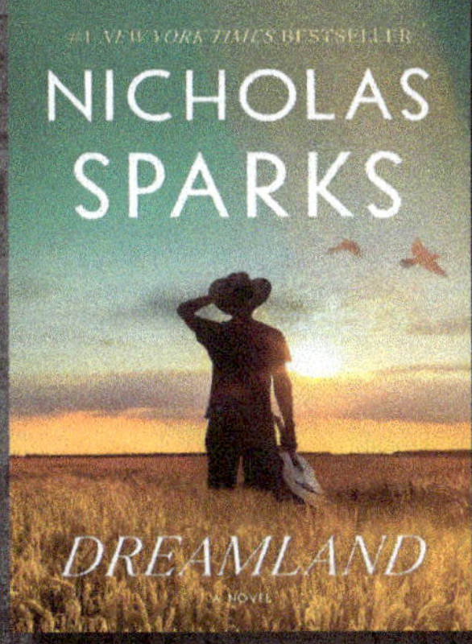

Dreamland
NICHOLAS SPARKS

"From this singular work it's clear that [Sparks] . . . continues to hone his craft."
—The Cullman Times

https://amzn.to/3Yx5tTR

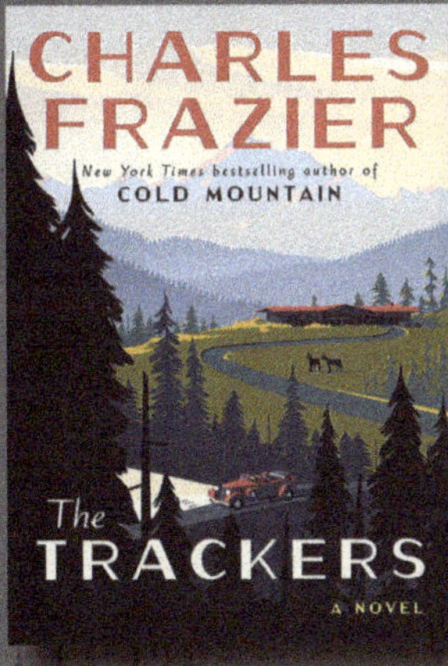

The Trackers
CHARLES FRAZIER

"Frazier is in top form.... Period-authentic, and the writing hums with spectacular word-images.... [A] propulsive tale of individualistic characters striving to beat the odds."
— Booklist (starred review)

https://amzn.to/3WwTWRJ

Horse
GERALDINE BROOKS

"[A] deft novel . . . create[s] a picture of the artistic, athletic, and scientific passions that horses can inspire in humans."
—The New Yorker

https://amzn.to/4d6exne

The Girl Who Survived
LISA JACKSON

This suspenseful thriller is packed with jaw-dropping twists."
—InTouch

https://amzn.to/3A0VUIR

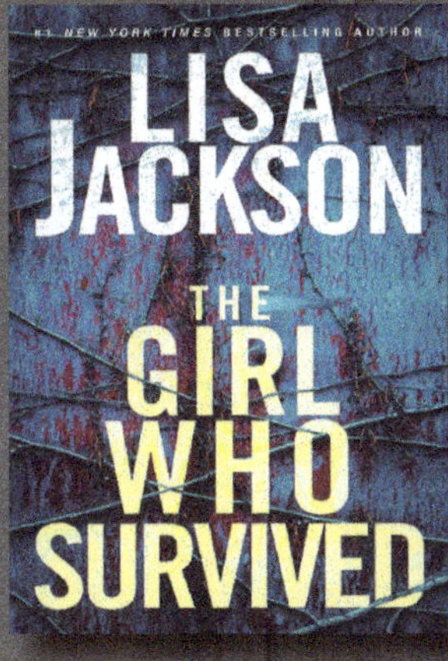

A Novel Summer
JAMIE BRENNER

"The perfect summer beach read! Rival bookshops, second chance romance, friend drama, it was the perfect book to curl up and escape to the Cape."
—Pamela Kelley, bestselling author of Bookshop by the Bay

https://amzn.to/3WtdCpF

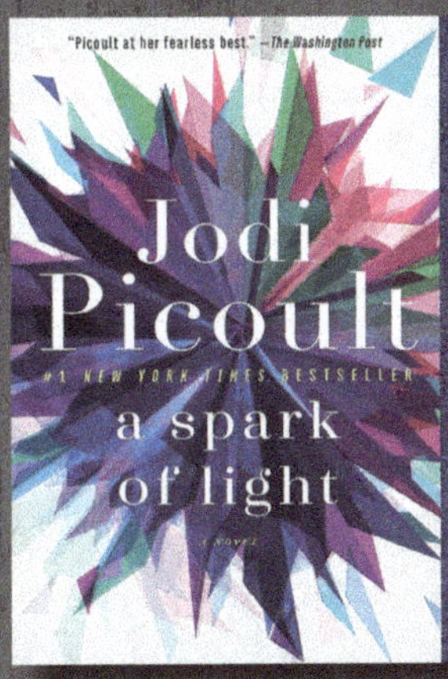

A Spark of Light
JODI PICOULT

"Picoult at her fearless best . . . Timely, balanced and certain to inspire debate."
—The Washington Post

https://amzn.to/3SzeesG

The Beekeeper of Aleppo
CHRISTY LEFTERI

"Beekeeper Nuri and his wife, Afra, are devastated by the Syrian civil war. After violence claims their child and Afra's eyesight, the couple is forced to flee Aleppo and make the fraught journey to Britain—and an uncertain future."
—USA Today

https://amzn.to/4dsnhnu

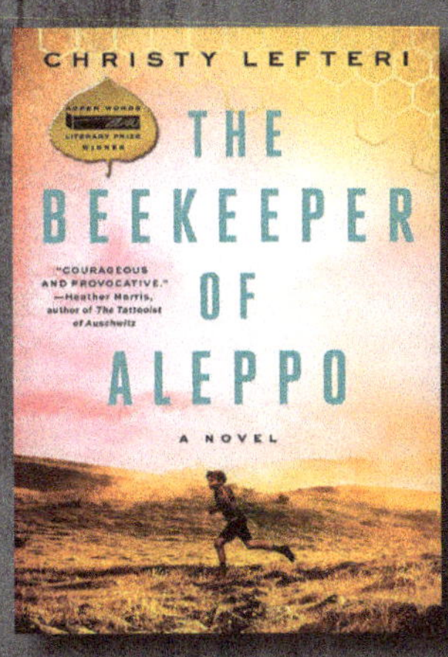

A Novel Love Story
ASHLEY POSTON

"Ashley Poston has written another clever, emotional love story part fantasy, part romcom—perfect for passing a day or three by the pool."
—Harper's Bazaar

https://amzn.to/3WKwcLt

CONTENTS

Secrets to Bestseller Success : A Chat withHeavyweights

Exclusive Interviews and Expert Advice from Award-Winning Authors.

Exploring the Life and Works of a Literary Sensation

Gregg Hurwitz

Master of Modern Thrillers

PUBLISHER: Novelist Post, A Subsidiary of Newyox Media. 200 Suite 134-146 Curtain Road, EC2A 3AR London
t: +44 79 3847 8420 editor@novelistpost.com II http://newyox.media
EDITORIAL: Ben F. Oncu, Editor-in-Chief, Ermesto Kara, Managing Editor, C. Rochelle, Art Editor, Delfina Reneta, Content Editor,
Editorial Desk: Adelina Alban, Carly Preston Carine O'Leary, Amy Stanford, M. Gunesen, Z. Robers CONTRIBUTOS: Claudine D. Reyes, Gary Fleder (cover photo), Adrian T.
We assume no responsibility for unsolicited manuscripts or art materials provided from our contributors.

EDITOR'S LETTER

Welcome to the third issue of *Novelist Post Magazine*! It is both a privilege and a delight to share this journey through the fascinating and ever-evolving world of storytelling with you. This issue marks yet another milestone in our commitment to spotlighting exceptional authors and celebrating the art of writing that continues to shape our lives and imaginations.

We are thrilled to feature Gregg Hurwitz on our cover—a literary titan whose gripping narratives, boundless creativity, and unyielding exploration of the human spirit have captivated audiences worldwide. Gregg's body of work spans bestselling novels, unforgettable comic book creations like *Batman* and *Wolverine*, screenwriting, and even poetry. With his *Orphan X* series, Gregg has given us a flawed, complex, and heroic protagonist who embodies the fight to remain human amidst a morally ambiguous world. Through an illuminating interview, Gregg delves into his creative process, the risks he's taken for research, and his perspective on everything from navigating moral themes in his thrillers to addressing cultural polarization with curiosity and empathy—a virtue we deeply admire in today's divided times.

This issue doesn't stop at Gregg Hurwitz. We've had the honor of conducting interviews with an incredible lineup of award-winning and bestselling authors who are masters in their craft and innovators in their respective genres. Ann Charles, Ann Zachariah, Anthony Bidulka, Brenda Stanley, Cassidy Carson, Catherine Ryan Hyde, Donna E. Lane, Donna McDonald, Gina Conroy, J.T. Hume, John Reinhardt, John Winn Miller, Marlene M. Bell, Lucinda Race, Ron Lamberson, Sirrah Medeiros, Sharon Varney, Sophie McKenzie, and Tracy Watland represent some of the finest voices in modern literature. From thrillers and romances to historical dramas and heartfelt tales of resilience, each author has their own unique approach to storytelling, inspired by their lives, passions, and dedication to their craft.

Here at *Novelist Post Magazine*, we celebrate storytellers who challenge our minds and stir our souls—authors who allow us to explore new worlds, perspectives, and emotions, all while inspiring us to dream a little bigger. It is this love for stories that connects us, transcending borders, languages, and time itself.

And speaking of timelessness, *Novelist Post* is available to you in print—always. We are proud to have our magazine reach readers in over 190 countries through thousands of platforms, including Amazon, Barnes & Noble, Waterstones, Blackwells, Indigo, AbeBooks, and many more. Regardless of how the world changes, our mission is to deliver the magic of storytelling, in tangible form, to your homes.

As you dive into this issue, I hope you'll find reflections, insights, and inspiration that ignite your passion for reading and writing. Whether you're an established author, a budding storyteller, or someone who simply loves the written word, this magazine is for you.

Thank you for being part of the *Novelist Post* family, and here's to many more chapters to come.

Happy reading,

Ben F. Oncu

CONT

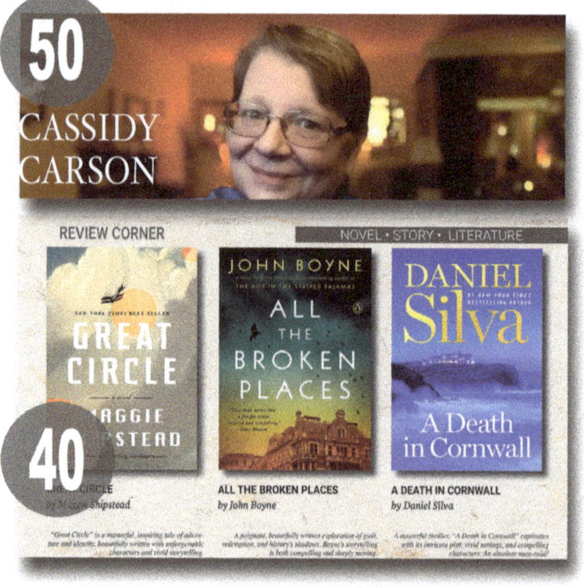
REVIEW CORNER
NOVEL • STORY • LITERATURE
GREAT CIRCLE
JOHN BOYNE
ALL THE BROKEN PLACES
DANIEL Silva
A Death in Cornwall
ALL THE BROKEN PLACES
by John Boyne
A DEATH IN CORNWALL
by Daniel Silva

ENTS

46 JOHN REINHARDT

58 Diane Pieri

ART & MEDIA

54 SHARON VARNEY

11 Eric Tillinghast

66 Januario Jano

60

Dr. Ann Zachariah Explores Writing, Healing And The Journey Of Self-Discovery

Dr. Ann Zachariah discusses her creative process, blending psychiatry and storytelling, focusing on emotional healing, authenticity, and the empowering transformation of pain into purpose through her diverse literary works.

BY NOVELIST POST STAFF

Emotional Connections In Literature

Dr. Ann Zachariah is a rare voice in literature, seamlessly blending her expertise as a psychiatrist with a gift for storytelling that resonates deeply across genres. Her works—spanning memoir, self-help, poetry, and fiction—offer readers solace, inspiration, and empowerment. Whether navigating grief, rediscovering personal strength, or exploring spiritual awakening, her books create safe spaces for emotional healing.

In her memoir, *Light Beyond the Veil*, Dr. Zachariah reflects on her father's passing with profound vulnerability, guiding readers toward their own paths of healing. Her book *Unlock Your Best Self & Conquer Grief* provides actionable tools to transform loss into personal growth, while her poetry collection, *Wild Child of the Monsoons*, captures raw human emotion with lyrical beauty. Even her fiction, such as T*he Invisible Red String*, delves into themes of connection and destiny that transcend cultural and emotional boundaries.

As both a psychiatrist and writer, Dr. Zachariah's approach is deeply compassionate, combining clinical wisdom with a heartfelt exploration of the human experience. Her works remind us of the power within to rise above pain, embrace our authentic selves, and find meaning amid life's challenges.

In this interview, Dr. Zachariah shares insights into her creative process, the themes that drive her writing, and her advice for aspiring authors seeking to write with authenticity and courage. Her books are a testament to the healing potential of words—and an invitation to discover their transformative power.

In Light Beyond the Veil, you blend personal grief with spiritual growth—what inspired you to share your father's passing so openly, and how did writing this memoir impact your own healing?

My overwhelming loss led me to understand that spiritual elements were necessary for my healing journey. In that healing process, the organic left brain's function was limited. My unfiltered story was shared because I believed it would help those who needed it. To do that, I needed to be completely transparent and unreserved.

Unlock Your Best Self & Conquer Grief offers seven strategies—was there one in particular that shifted your perspective most profoundly while writing?

Yes, often overlooked is the importance of honoring the loss. To keep going, we repress our sadness. Unless we acknowledge and accept our grief, we cannot move on from it.

In From Heartbreak to Healing: OMG! I JUST GOT GHOSTED, you explore ghosting—what psychological insight do you hope readers gain most from this book?

Briefly, your being ghosted isn't about you. You are not to blame.

Your poetry in Wild Child of the Monsoons captures raw emotion—how does writing poetry differ emotionally from your self-help and memoir work?

Poetry is the dance of your dreams and the song of your soul. It frequently originates from your higher self.

The Invisible Red String weaves themes of destiny and cross-cultural connection—what real-life experiences influenced this story?

My childhood spanned three continents, immersing me in their diverse cultures. I infused my characters with unique colors by incorporating diverse cultural elements.

As a psychiatrist and author, how do you integrate clinical expertise into emotional guidance across your books?

I weave my clinical expertise into emotional guidance, often using storytelling. Stories filled with love and guidance touch the deepest parts of our hearts.

Looking across your work—memoir, poetry, self-help, fiction—what common thread do you feel ties them all together?

Personal empowerment, spiritual awakening and consciousness expansion

The underlying theme in all my writings is a gentle invitation for readers to recognize their own power and divinity, encouraging them to love themselves and create a life rooted in healing rather than past wounds

What advice would you give aspiring authors who wish to write authentically about personal pain and transformation?

Just as your voice expresses your unique vibration, your writing reflects it too. When you write with love and authenticity, you tap into your divine power, connecting with the hearts and minds of those seeking your unique message. Always write from your heart.

Dr. Zachariah's literary brilliance combines emotional depth, clinical insight, and inspiration, empowering readers to embrace healing, spirituality, and personal growth.

Writing is a reflection of our innermost thoughts—a journey into our vulnerabilities and strengths."

Ann Zachariah

Exploring Water, Sculpture, And Cultural Connections

Eric Tillinghast's art, shaped by nature and technical expertise, transforms water into sculpture, connecting universal themes with cultural perspectives, and creating evocative works celebrated across international galleries and public spaces.

Eric Tillinghast, a Los Angeles-based artist, has been profoundly influenced by the diverse landscapes of California, where he grew up surrounded by the wide-open spaces and natural beauty of Mount Shasta. His artistic journey, chronicled in an interview with WOWwART magazine, reveals a deep connection to nature and a unique approach to materials that have shaped his creations.

Tillinghast, born in Los Angeles in 1974, spent his formative years in Northern California, an experience that ingrained in him a lasting appreciation for the natural world—particularly water. This early exposure to lakes and rivers has had a significant impact on his body of work, where water plays a central role as both material and subject. As Tillinghast explains, his fascination with water as an element encourages viewers to revisit personal memories and experiences, fostering a connection that resonates differently across cultural contexts.

In an effort to broaden his skill set, Tillinghast pursued industrial welding, acquiring a formal education in the craft in Santa Barbara. This technical background has been instrumental in his creation of large-scale sculptures and installations. The precision and mastery of metalworking have enabled him to translate his conceptual visions into tangible forms, seamlessly merging technique with artistic expression.

Tillinghast's works have garnered international attention, with exhibitions spanning prestigious venues such as The Albright Knox Gallery, The Long Beach Museum of Art, and the Center for Contemporary Art in Santa Fe, among others. His pieces invoke varied interpretations worldwide, a testament to the universal yet culturally specific experiences of water within the different communities they reach. Cultural history, mythology, and geographic factors all play roles in coloring the perceptions of his installations, which, as Tillinghast notes, are always received distinctively from one locale to another.

Site-specific installations hold a particular allure for Tillinghast. These projects represent a dynamic interplay between the artwork and its environment, where the characteristics of the site itself—from architecture to natural light—inform the creative process. He approaches such spaces as partners in creation, meticulously examining how elements like sunlight will interact with water and reflective surfaces. This attention to environmental detail guides his selection of sites that naturally complement and enhance the visual and experiential impact of his work.

Public art projects, while offering expansive possibilities, present their own set of challenges. Tillinghast has navigated complex collaborations involving clients, architects, engineers, and city officials, often requiring lengthy negotiations and approvals. Despite the bureaucratic complexities, these endeavors allow him to achieve creative heights that are unfeasible within the confines of a traditional studio setting. Large-scale public installations grant him the freedom to explore bold concepts that resonate across vast spaces, making art a shared, communal experience.

Over his illustrious career, Tillinghast's innovative use of water and metal has earned him recognition from prestigious institutions such as The Pollock-Krasner Foundation and the Dallas Museum of Art. His commitment to exploring the intersection of nature and technology continues to captivate audiences, inviting them to engage with art in transformative ways that reflect the rich tapestry of cultural and individual perspectives.

Source: WOWwART magazine interview with Eric Tillinghast.

> *"Spending a lot of time around lakes and rivers during my childhood influenced my art significantly."*

Eric Tillinghast Draws Inspiration from Nature and Craftsmanship to Create Water-Inspired Art

Art & Culture

Eric Tillinghast, a master of water-inspired art, blends nature and technical craftsmanship to craft thought-provoking sculptures and installations.

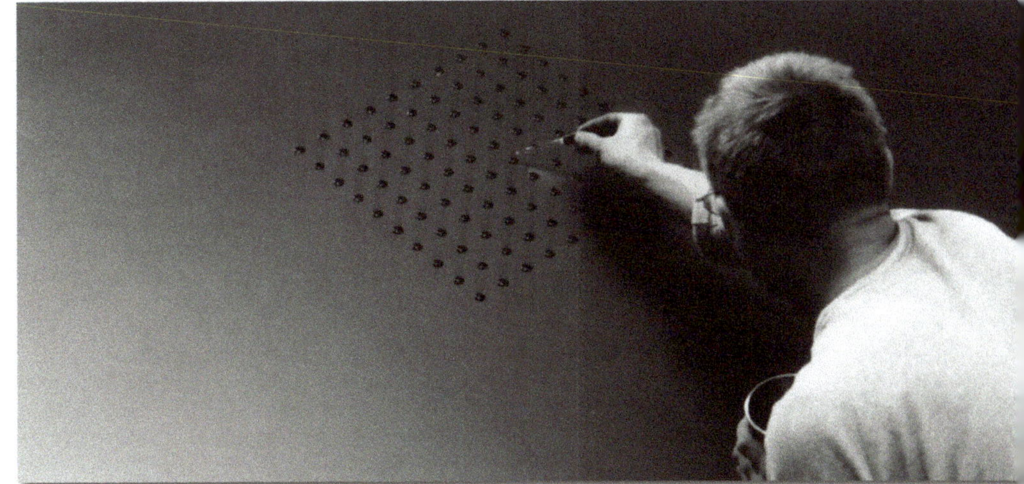

-ric Tillinghast

Marlene M. Bell Weaves Romantic Mystery and Sheep Into Enthralling Novels

Marlene M. Bell masterfully blends mystery, romance, and deeply personal experiences to craft award-winning novels and children's books, all enriched by her artistry, photography, and passion for sheep.

PHOTO: Award-Winning Author Marlene M. Bell Shares How Life, Art, and Passion Inspire Her Creative Writing Journey

Championing The Art Of Storytelling

by Carly Preston

There are few authors whose creativity spans across such diverse genres and art forms with the seamless grace of Marlene M. Bell. A masterful storyteller, she has garnered accolades for her Annalisse series of romantic mysteries, which consistently capture the imagination with their international intrigue, dynamic suspense, and powerful emotional depth. Bell's beautifully detailed prose reflects her rich background as an artist and photographer, painting scenes so vivid they immerse readers completely in her intricately woven narratives. Her love for antiquities, history, and compelling characters shines through in every twist and turn of her stories.

But Bell's versatility doesn't stop there. From thrilling mysteries to heartfelt children's books, she knows how to engage readers of all ages. Her award-winning children's book, *Mia and Nattie: One Great Team*, is a heartwarming true story inspired by her own experiences raising sheep on her picturesque East Texas ranch. It's impossible not to be captivated by the sense of love and loyalty that infuses this tale, much like the life she shares with her woolly companions.

Marlene's work, whether set against the backdrop of New Zealand's breathtaking landscapes or the small-town charm of rural East Texas, merges her personal passions with rich, evocative storytelling. With her ability to balance suspense, romance, history, and culture, she creates worlds where readers lose themselves while forming deep emotional connections to her characters. In this exclusive interview, Marlene shares the inspirations, challenges, and personal experiences behind her writing journey, providing a glimpse into the heart and mind of one of today's most multifaceted storytellers. Prepare to be inspired.

What inspired you to include sheep as characters or subject matter in your books?

It's easier to "write what you know." With each new series installment or standalone mystery, there is always a fair amount of research involved for subject matter I'm unfamiliar with, such as describing countries I haven't visited. Raising livestock for over forty years has become second-nature for me, and I make sure that my protagonists have a soft spot for sheep because that life is a part of me. In Annalisse series book #4, Copper Waters, I had the opportunity to add a little about sheep husbandry in the story due to the New Zealand location and its lovely environment.

How has your experience as an artist and photographer influenced your writing style?

My artistic abilities have made me a better writer, I think. I adore painting visual pictures in text for my readers by placing each person in the chapter. Deep descriptions of the surroundings and sometimes relying on sensory details make the reading experience more enjoyable. Taking local photographs and looking at photos from seaside locations, as an example, help to portray a sense of what my characters see, and how they feel in these scenes.

Can you share a behind-the-scenes story about writing "Copper Waters"?

During the drafting of Copper Waters, I recalled an event from a personal experience while innocently working around the Suffolk stud ram on our ranch. This near-miss incident helped me craft one of the casualties near the barn in Copper Waters. My husband's warning, "never turn your back on a ram" was the basis for the scene with the ranch manager in this novel.

My experience: While trimming trees from inside the pasture where the sheep were grazing, I had my back to the sheep and forgot about our ram in the group. Rams are especially territorial during breeding season. By the time I realized Zeus the ram was stalking me, he was mid-stride, charging my wheelbarrow. When I turned to face him, I was forced to run backward pulling a wheelbarrow heavy in foliage. My boot heel caught a divot in the ground, and down I went. I remember looking up at Zeus towering over me. My husband intervened and managed to distract the ram so that I could stand and leave the paddock. For the ranch manager in Copper Waters, a disaster occurs.

What's the most challenging aspect of blending mystery with romance in the Annalisse series?

The biggest challenge is setting up a realistic scene for the reader. I ask myself if Annalisse and Alec's romantic encounters are believable during the constant peril they face from multiple villains. Will some readers consider scenes too far-fetched and keep reading anyway? My goal is to balance it all. Writing international adventures while offsetting a love story element, is tricky business. Blending multiple

> Marlene M. Bell's storytelling is captivating and authentic, seamlessly merging vivid creativity, relatable characters, and heartfelt connections that resonate with readers of all ages.

genres in the Annalisse series takes more thought than a standalone mystery with one focus. Even though my novels are fiction, the reader has to believe the stories are plausible.

How did true events from your sheep ranch shape "Mia and Nattie: One Great Team!"?

Raising a lamb in the home has happened only once in our long career with sheep. Natalie was special and almost human because we raised her away from the flock. The day she had to go out with them was as hard on us as it was for her. Because Natalie was born so tiny, and we had zero success bottle-feeding lambs that small previously, my husband wasn't convinced she would survive. Nattie had the will to live, and in my opinion, that saved her. From a three-pound miracle of survival, she had a special place to wander around the home for thirteen years. Mia and Nattie One Great Team portrays me as Mia, Nattie as herself, and the difficult grandmother in the story is my husband—who had to come around in the end and see things from my point of view. The children's book is our true story in every respect.

What led you to write a standalone cozy mystery like "A Hush at Midnight"?

The challenge of trying something else. Following Copper Waters, I thought a standalone mystery might be a nice break from a whirlwind series installment. Still crime and still a mystery, but with no gory details and less romance. Cozies also move more slowly. Now that I've written A Hush at Midnight, my series readers seem to be on the fence about the genre after reading the faster moving Annalisse series. Although A Hush at Midnight has won many book awards, I prefer the faster pacing of the chase.

How do you balance suspense and character development in your romantic mystery novels?

Similarly to the balancing act of romance and mystery. I try to write a believable story while having each character be true to themselves. The suspenseful story comes naturally, if I've plotted the outline well. My characters tend to speak to me or guide me as I write, which helps.

What inspired you to create the cursed jewelry storyline in "Stolen Obsession"?

Stolen Obsession has actual historical elements in it. Because I'm an avid fan of antiquities and strange history, these things were a must for my first work of fiction. Many relics carry interesting backstories with them. The events I created in book one use real Persian history as the basis for a curse that sends diabolical evil barreling toward my characters.

Can you discuss the process of crafting the small-town secrets in "A Hush at Midnight"?

Secrets come naturally when one has a creative mind. I tend to write what's familiar to me, and find it enjoyable to add a few quirky elements of personal stories to craft my novels. Living in small towns throughout California to East Texas where Hush takes place, rural community personalities come alive in A Hush at Midnight because of the generosity and uniqueness of native Texans.

How do real locations and cultures influence the exotic settings in your stories?

As a rule, I take small bits of fact and blend it with fiction when writing settings in my novels. I like to use fictitious names for towns, yet leave the general areas intact for countries easy to find on a world map. As in Copper Waters, the Māori culture is prevalent in this story because they are indigenous to the region. I believe that weaving fact with fiction makes for a more interesting and enlightening read.

> Marlene M. Bell delivers an engaging, suspense-filled cozy mystery with *A Hush at Midnight.* Twists abound as Laura Harris fights to clear her name, unveiling shocking secrets and danger. Bell's vivid characters and small-town intrigue keep readers guessing until the final reveal. A must-read for fans of clever, tightly woven mysteries.

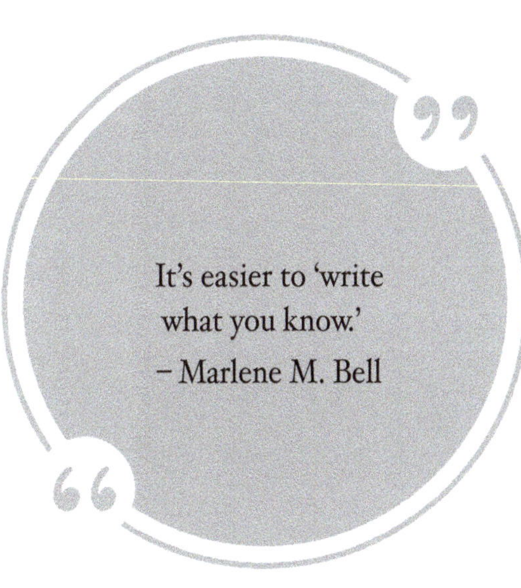

Award-Winning Author Shares Her Creative Journey and Inspirations

Lucinda Race Blends Cozy Mysteries and Romance with Heart, Hope and Paranormal Charm

Lucinda Race discusses her writing process, blending paranormal elements with cozy mysteries, creating relatable characters, and crafting emotionally rich stories inspired by her life and travels.

LUCINDA RACE
BREATHE
Price Family Romance Series

Lucinda Race's *Breathe* delivers a heartfelt small-town romance. Tessa Price's determination to revive the struggling Sand Creek Winery and prove her worth is both inspiring and compelling. The chemistry between Tessa and Max Maxwell, the former owner with a brooding charm, builds naturally, weaving tension and tenderness into their partnership. As secrets unearth and emotions deepen, the story balances romance, resilience, and family dynamics beautifully. With its rich vineyard setting and emotional stakes, this first installment in the Price Family Romance Series offers a flavorful blend of passion and hope. Perfect for fans of small-town love!

by Carine O'Leary

Lucinda Race's literary world is a treasure trove of emotion, imagination, and endearing characters that draw readers into heartfelt romances and captivating mysteries. With a talent for crafting tales brimming with intrigue and joy, Lucinda has become a beacon of inspiration in the literary community. Her ability to create small-town settings that feel as familiar as home—yet packed with surprises around every corner—underscores her mastery of storytelling.

Through her beloved McKenna Family Romance series and her uniquely enchanting Paranormal Cozy Nook Bookstore series, Lucinda skillfully fuses the sweetness of clean romance with the thrill of suspenseful murder plots. The charm of her writing lies in her versatility—whether it's a talking familiar in a cozy mystery or the emotional depth of finding love later in life, Lucinda's stories appeal to readers of all ages and genres.

As you read this exclusive Novelist Post interview, you'll glimpse the creative brilliance and personal warmth that make Lucinda Race not only a celebrated author but also a cherished voice in contemporary fiction. From inspiration drawn from her adorable canine companions to her insights on blending emotions and mystery, Lucinda's journey is as captivating as the books she creates. It's a privilege to share her thoughts and experiences with our readers, and we think you'll agree—her stories leave an indelible mark on the heart.

What inspired you to blend paranormal elements with cozy mysteries in your Book Store Cozy Mystery series?

I love reading paranormal cozy mysteries, and adding those elements gives an author a broader license for creativity.

How do you balance the sweet, clean romance themes with suspenseful murder plots in your writing?

I would like to have anyone at any age read these books so keeping them sweet in the romance department and non-violent despite they're murder mystery books is the best avenue to success.

Which of your fictional characters do you personally relate to the most, and why?

Milo, the talking familiar, is fashioned after our former family cat, Mordy. I could always picture Mordy talking in a snarky but loving attitude.

How does living in western Massachusetts influence the small-town settings in your books?

Small town life means you recognize faces, family names and gasp, "you heard he did what?" kind of thing. Small towns are mini universe until themselves which again adds to the gasp factor in cozy mystery books.

What challenges have you faced transitioning from nonfiction writing to fiction?

Writing fiction is so much easier. :) I can have characters to what I want, say and act according to my muse. Its a wonderful thing. Non-fiction, is based in facts and its difficult to make technical documents interesting. There's no room for humor.

How do you develop the emotional depth in your later-in-life romance stories like Lost and Found?

I'm an older woman who has been blessed to experience love a second time. My personal life had "all the feels" and I wanted to bring that to life in my work.

Can you share your process for building series arcs that allow each book to also stand alone?

Elements connect the books as the series, such as family dynamics and the small town the books take place in. However, I try to write a book that has a satisfactory story arc of its

Lucinda Race's storytelling captivates with warmth, humor, and imaginative tales, making her a cherished voice in romance and cozy mysteries.

Lucinda Race, surrounded by inspiration, pens heartwarming tales in the hills of western Massachusetts.

own. But, getting to know the other characters provides depth to the reading experience.

Which book or series was the most fun for you to write and what made it special?

That's like asking which is my favorite child. They're all special. For romance, I loved writing Price Family Romance Series. It was a spinoff from Ready to Soar and set in a winery in the Finger Lakes region of New York. My husband and I traveled there with friends and it was so enjoyable, it made the perfect setting for this series. And a new book in that series will be released in 2026. Stella Maxwell is finally getting her happily ever after.

How do you keep your ideas fresh after writing so many series and standalone novels?

Prior to becoming a full-time writer, I traveled for my day job. Sitting in airports and at conventions I was fortunate to observe people, and I always made up little stories about them, where did they live, family, dating, spouses, career choices, that kind of thing. I let my imagination come out to play and stories simmered. I have a pretty good memory so recall to certain locations, people and emotions come back when I'm ready to write them.

What advice would you give to aspiring authors who want to craft both mystery and romance into their stories?

Don't let what the rules say you can and can't do. For a long time I thought I couldn't write cozy and cross over since I was a romance author. But when I tossed away the rule book my creativity was unleashed. Just write what your muse is urging you to write. I promise, it's liberating.

I love reading paranormal cozy mysteries, and adding those elements gives an author a broader license for creativity."

Lucinda Race

The Power Of Family, History, And Humanity

Brenda Stanley masterfully intertwines suspense and emotional depth in *It Happened in the Hollow*. This hauntingly beautiful novel explores grief, guilt, and the power of human connection as Landis and Benji navigate the secrets hidden within the Idaho woods. Stanley's vivid descriptions bring the setting to life, while the dual perspectives of the living and the dead add an intriguing layer of complexity. With compelling characters and a gripping mystery, this story is both poignant and thrilling, leaving readers captivated until the very last page. A must-read for fans of soulful suspense.

Brenda Stanley Inspires Readers Through Suspense, Secrets, And Emotional Connections

Author Brenda Stanley shares her creative journey, blending suspense, emotional depth, and personal experiences to craft gripping novels and explore themes of family, secrets, and resilience with authenticity.

By Novelist Post Staff

Brenda Stanley is, without question, a literary force to be reckoned with—a writer whose extraordinary talent defies boundaries and genres. With suspenseful plots that keep readers on edge and emotionally complex characters that leave lasting impressions, her novels are the kind of stories you carry with you long after the final page. Drawing inspiration from her dynamic life experiences—whether as a tenacious investigative journalist, an Idaho ranch owner, or a mother navigating the intricacies of a large family—Brenda seamlessly blends authenticity, depth, and intrigue into every book she writes.

Brenda Stanley, an author whose works reveal the profound humanity nestled within the darkest secrets and the resilience found in even the most fragile connections. As Brenda shares the fascinating journey behind her craft, including the inspiration for her upcoming novel *It Happened in the Hollow*, readers will gain insight into the boundless curiosity and heartfelt passion that make her stories resonate so deeply. Brenda Stanley is not just a storyteller; she's an architect of emotion, and her ability to weave together mystery, history, and human connection is nothing short of remarkable. This interview is not to be missed.

What inspired you to start writing novels, and how did you develop your style of incorporating suspense and mystery?

I have always loved to read and that inspired my desire to write. My father worked in law enforcement and as an undercover agent for the DEA. This shaped my writing style by instilling a strong sense of suspense, attention to detail, and a fascination with the hidden motives behind people's actions.

How has your background as a television news anchor and investigative reporter influenced your approach to storytelling?

My career as an investigative journalist taught me how to dig beneath the surface, ask the right questions, and tell compelling, fact-driven stories. That experience shaped my fiction by giving me a strong sense of pacing, character motivation, and how to weave suspense through real-world details that make a story feel authentic and urgent.

Can you share your experience of writing your first novel at the age of seventeen and how it shaped your journey as an author?

When I wrote my first novel, I was a teen mom. I was living in a very rural and isolated part of Utah, and reading and writing were what I did to escape the loneliness and uncertainty of that time. Writing became my refuge—a way to process everything I was going through and to imagine a world beyond my immediate reality.

What elements of life in Idaho and your small ranch inspire your settings and characters?

Many of my stories evolve from what I see and experience here in Idaho and on my own property. I love to ride horses in the mountains and hike in the woods. My stories often feature these elements. My most recent novel even incorporates fly fishing into the storyline.

How do you balance creating intriguing suspenseful plots with the emotional depth of your characters?

For me, the key to balancing suspense with emotional depth is making sure the plot serves the characters, not the other way around. I start with people—flawed, complex, and real—and let their fears, secrets, and desires drive the tension. Suspense isn't just about what's happening; it's about why it matters to the characters, when readers care about who's at the center of the storm, every twist and reveal hits that much harder.

What was the creative process like for your upcoming book, "It Happened in the Hollow," and what inspired the story?

I wanted to tell this story from two perspectives—one grounded in the present, and one looking in from beyond the veil. That structure allowed me to weave together past and present, showing how long-buried truths still shape the lives unfolding now. I spent a considerable amount of time researching Idaho's history, particularly the rivers and waterways that serve as the state's lifeblood. It's not just fiction—people have truly been killed over land and water rights. Fly fishing became the perfect vehicle to connect two generations with the river.

How do your personal experiences, such as being a mother of five and your connection to family, influence the themes in your novels?

Being a mother of five has deeply shaped the way I write about relationships, resilience, and the bonds that hold us together, even when they're messy or strained. Family, in all its complexity, is at the heart

Brenda Stanley: Masterfully weaving mystery, history, and emotion, the acclaimed author captivates readers with unforgettable characters and gripping, suspenseful narratives.

Brenda Stanley's storytelling brilliance lies in her ability to balance suspense and humanity, leaving readers captivated by her emotionally resonant novels.

of my stories. I'm especially drawn to the impact of family secrets—how what's hidden or unspoken can echo through generations. My personal experience helps me write characters who love fiercely, fight hard, and carry both joy and pain with them, just like real families do, especially when the past refuses to stay buried.

What challenges do you face in maintaining uniqueness and creativity in your various novels?

One of the biggest challenges is ensuring that each story feels fresh while remaining true to my voice. I never want to repeat a plot or character arc just because it worked before. To keep things unique, I dig deeper into new themes, settings, or emotional truths I haven't explored yet. It also helps to stay curious about people, history, and even my own fears. Creativity comes from simply asking, What if?

How do you approach weaving intricate and mysterious storylines without giving away too much too soon?

I approach it like a puzzle—revealing just enough pieces at a time to keep readers curious, but not so much that they can see the whole picture too early. I also write my endings first, so I know where my story is leading, and it helps me keep the complex twists from deviating from where I need them to go. It's all about timing and perspective. I use character emotions, setting, and subtle clues to build tension, trusting the reader to pick up on what's between the lines. Holding back just the right details creates that sense of unease and anticipation that makes a mystery compelling.

What advice would you give to aspiring authors who want to write compelling and emotionally resonant stories?

Write the story that scares you a little—the one that feels personal, vulnerable, or deeply honest. That's where the emotional resonance lives. Don't be afraid to dig into your own experiences and truths, because authenticity is what makes a story stick with readers. Also, spend time getting to know your characters; the more real they feel to you, the more real they'll feel to others.

Suspense isn't just about what's happening; it's about why it matters to the characters."

Brenda Stanley

Exploring Love, Laughter, And Lifelong Creativity

Donna McDonald Shares How Humor, Strong Heroines And Resilience Shape Her Remarkable Multi-Genre Writing Journey

Donna McDonald, USA Today Bestselling Author, discusses her multi-genre writing journey, creative process, resilience after personal loss, and her commitment to crafting strong heroines and relatable, joyful romances.

By Novelist Post Staff

Donna McDonald's *Never Is A Very Long Time* is a delightful romantic comedy packed with humor, heart, and relatable characters. Dr. Mariah Bates navigates love, heartbreak, and reinvention with charm and resilience, making readers cheer for her every step of the way. With witty banter, laugh-out-loud moments, and a sprinkle of rekindled hope, this vibrant story celebrates finding love later in life. Perfect for readers craving romance with real-life challenges and plenty of laughs!

Donna McDonald is the quintessential storyteller who reminds us all that it's never too late to answer the call of creativity. With over a decade of publishing success and nearly one hundred books to her name, she has captivated readers across a spectrum of genres—from swoon-worthy contemporary romances to adrenaline-packed science fiction and paranormal tales. Donna's signature blend of humor, heart, and relatable heroines has solidified her place not only as a USA Today Bestselling Author but as a beloved voice that dares to challenge genre conventions and societal norms.

Dubbed the queen of mature romance, Donna brings life to characters who often go overlooked in traditional narratives—proving that love, adventure, and personal growth don't come with an expiration date. Whether she's crafting heartbreakingly human cyborg soldiers, tenacious action heroines, or independent, witty women navigating love later in life, Donna's ability to infuse both depth and levity into her stories is unmatched. Through her heartwarming and hilarious tales, she's taught her readers not just to believe in second chances, but to revel in them.

In this exclusive interview, we delve into the life and mind behind the stories. Donna opens up about how a personal tragedy became the spark for her writing career, the importance of laughter in fiction, and her philosophy on creating complex worlds and even more complex characters. Get ready to be inspired by an author who doesn't just write happy endings—she builds them, one story at a time.

What inspired you to start writing romance novels after a long career in other fields?

I'm a voracious reader and have always been a writer of some sort. Regardless of how I made money, publishing a book remained on my "to-do-one-day" list. I wish I could say I made it happen by simply sitting down to write, but that wasn't the case. In 2009, my oldest daughter was diagnosed with stage four cancer. I took care of her during the last year of her life and didn't recover quickly from her loss. A few months after she died, I started writing. Weeks later, I discovered I had written 75,000 words. It was a bittersweet triumph to finally type "The End" and know it was a complete, finished story. You could say writing rescued me from my grief, and you wouldn't be wrong. I prefer writing fiction with happily-ever-after or happy-for-now endings because real life does not offer those to everyone. I enjoy having the power to create them in my fiction.

How do you balance humor with romance in your stories to keep readers engaged?

Love and romance are essential elements in most successful stories. Humor can provide a chance to breathe during tense conflicts. Also, laughter heals. A character with a quirky sense of humor is fun, and rooting for them is natural and easy. My readers love my stories because they know I will leave them smiling, no matter what happens in the plot. Bad things do happen in my fiction, but the good guys always win—always. If someone wants stark reality, the news can provide that. I prefer to grant wishes for my struggling characters and offer my readers a mental escape into a world where life works out.

Can you share how your "writer vacation" into science fiction and paranormal romance evolved into a full-fledged passion?

Initially, I aspired to write science fiction, paranormal, and fantasy stories. Female action and adventure characters were, and remain, relatively uncommon outside of Urban Fantasy and Paranormal Romance. You don't find many mature, kick-butt heroines in "mainstream" novels. When I first started publishing in 2011, I decided my contemporary romances with older characters would best set me apart in the indie author world. I defied the norms and wrote sexy, love-drenched, sensual romances with older characters. Back then, I would tell my contemporary readers that they would have to wait a bit for their next book because I was writing a science fiction story. I referred to it as my "writing vacation" because I thought they would understand that best. Variety is critical to my creativity.

What challenges do you face when creating believable romantic relationships involving complex sci-fi or paranormal elements?

World-building in science fiction and fantasy novels requires readers to suspend their normal beliefs to fully enjoy the story. My job is to make it worth a reader's time to believe that my scientifically created werewolves use nanotechnology to survive shifting, while they remain human enough to want to find love. When I wrote my cyborg series, the focus was on restoring each cyber soldier's humanity, with all that entails. I try to align my "science fiction" as closely with reality as possible for relatability. That is not possible with werewolves and dragons, so I don't bother to do that in fantasies.

How has your own life experience influenced your decision to write about older characters finding love?

Trite but true, it was me just writing about what I knew. I was fifty-two when I published my first novel. My first

contemporary romance heroine was turning fifty and wondering if life had passed her by. She was a divorced businesswoman with an adult daughter. She ran a business, had assistants, and still made time for her friends. Why wouldn't I want to write about a woman that strong and unstoppable? Sex, romance, and love do not suddenly end at thirty-five. Never Too Late is not just my first series title. It's my mantra for living my life.

What has been the most rewarding feedback you've received from readers about your portrayal of mature romance?

This list is lengthy because I have the best readers in the world, but I will focus on the top few. Some readers wrote to say my older characters inspired them to date again after losing a spouse, giving up, or surviving a horrific illness. Some wrote to say they read my work while keeping vigil at the side of a hospitalized loved one, and I lightened their hearts with my humor. Others mentioned they enjoyed reading an author who always made them laugh. The money I earn from sales enables me to continue writing, but these messages from readers are the actual proof of my success.

How do you develop strong, relatable heroines who also fit into humorous romantic comedies?

My characters are relatable because I find most people fascinating. Long before I met my humor-writing friend, I wanted to learn to craft humor. I had no money for formal classes, so I pulled out my favorite "chick flick" romantic comedies and turned on the director's cut. Nora Ephron and Nancy Meyers became my teachers. They discussed "in this scene..." and explained their choices. I took notes on timing, character development, and flow. Afterward, I wrote scenes and then went back and added what I thought of as "the funny" parts.

Could you explain your creative process for world-building in your science fiction romance series?

One book is never enough to tell the entire story my mind imagines, especially when showing character development through a variety of character-building experiences. Series are just natural for me. When I begin a new series, little movies featuring the newly created main character run through my mind. If the characters are happy with themselves and me, the mind movies multiply and connect to others. Before I know it, I'm immersed in the new world and become obsessed with finding words for it.

What advice do you have for authors who want to write across multiple genres without losing their unique voice?

I have no advice. If they end up needing to write across genres, as I did, I can only wish them the best of luck. I'm living a happy, creative life as a multi-genre author, but from a business standpoint, there is no doubt that I traded profit for creativity. Following my muse sounds noble, and it occasionally feels courageous, but it won't pay the bills unless I work tirelessly to sell each genre to the proper audience.

What is the most important piece of advice you would give to aspiring romance authors starting their writing journey?

Write the books of your heart because those stories will naturally resonate with the right readers. I'm preparing to release my one hundredth book

. I know that writing this one will be just as enjoyable as writing the first. Writing is my life, and I aim to create books until the end of my days. I would advise them not to forget to celebrate each book because every book deserves its own moment to shine, just as its author does.

> *Writing rescued me from my grief, and you wouldn't be wrong.*

Donna McDonald
USA TODAY BESTSELLİNG AUTHO

Lessons From A Literary Journey That Spans Decades

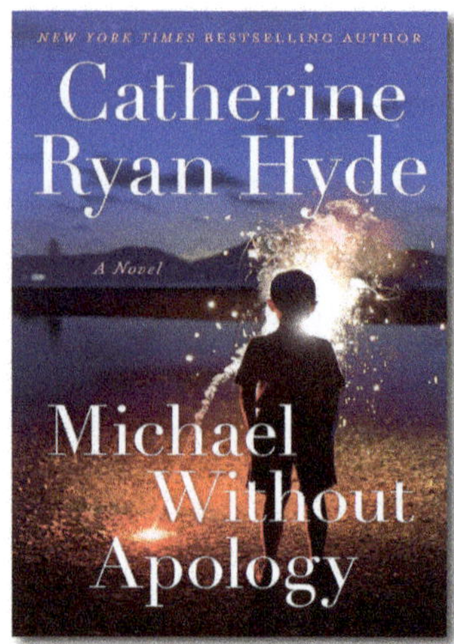

Catherine Ryan Hyde's *Michael Without Apology* is an emotionally resonant and deeply human story about trauma, resilience, and the transformative power of vulnerability. Michael's journey from shame to self-acceptance is beautifully portrayed, as he opens himself up through film, connecting with others battling their own insecurities. Hyde's nuanced exploration of body image, societal perceptions, and family abandonment feels raw and universal, reminding readers of our shared struggles. With poignant characters and deft storytelling, this novel is a powerful testament to healing and the courage it takes to embrace ourselves, unapologetically.

Catherine Ryan Hyde On Creativity, Resilience And The Enduring Power Of Storytelling

Catherine Ryan Hyde reflects on her journey of storytelling, sharing insights on perseverance, self-acceptance, animal companions, and how human connection inspires her deeply personal and universal narratives.

By Novelist Post Staff

Few authors possess the ability to touch hearts, ignite inspiration, and delve into the human experience with the authenticity and depth of Catherine Ryan Hyde. It is an honor to bring her voice to the pages of *Novelist Post*. With over fifty published works to her name, including the beloved classic *Pay It Forward*, Catherine has firmly established herself as a literary force, captivating readers worldwide with her contemplative storytelling and unflinching exploration of what it means to persevere with grace.

Her novels draw us into the lives of unforgettable characters—flawed, hopeful, and richly human—while her short stories, acclaimed in prestigious journals like *The Antioch Review* and *Ploughshares*, affirm her as a masterful storyteller across formats. Catherine's work transcends borders, translated into dozens of languages and embraced across continents. From her Lambda Literary Award-winning works to international bestsellers like *When I Found You* and *Walk Me Home*, her diverse repertoire is nothing short of extraordinary.

Yet perhaps what makes Catherine particularly inspiring isn't just her prolific career, impressive accolades, or her global reach—it's her steadfast commitment to staying true to the art of storytelling. Even as *Pay It Forward* became a cultural phenomenon and movie milestone, she reminds us that literature itself is the powerful heartbeat behind any legacy worth celebrating. Whether dreaming up characters who find redemption in the face of adversity or drawing inspiration from the quiet beauty of hiking trails and photography, Catherine infuses every page with sincerity, wisdom, and discovery.

In this intimate interview, Catherine opens up about the personal trials that have shaped her writing, the grace she's found in self-acceptance, and how themes of compassion, resilience, and redemption inform so many of her characters. For readers—and aspiring writers—seeking solace and direction, Catherine Ryan Hyde emerges not just as a bestselling author, but as a testament to the enduring power of creativity and connection.

What inspired you to write "Pay It Forward," and did you expect it to have such a profound impact globally?

I say the following with great respect to everyone who cares about that book. I hope it's received in that same spirit. I wrote that book in the mid-1990s. About 30 years ago. It was published 25 years ago, and I've published almost 50 more books since. While I appreciate the fact that people still care about it after all this time, it's harder for me to hold my attention on it. Some of that springs from the fact that you can only tell a story about a book just so many thousands of times. Mostly I think I'm discouraged by the fact that it seems to stand head and shoulders above all my other books in people's minds because it was a movie. Unfortunately, we live in a world where movies are considered more valuable than books. And yet I'm sticking with books.

That said, I do know there are many who love the book and the concept for itself, and for very good reasons.

On the Pay It Forward book detail page of my website I have a video of me telling the story of the inspiration behind the book. I put it there years ago and refer people to it because I couldn't bring myself to tell it one more time. And I mean that more literally than you might think.

As to the second question, no. I never imagined. I was a new and under-published author at the time. I had trouble even imagining it for sale in a book store.

How does your love for hiking and photography influence your writing?

I think it creates a space for my imagination to flow. And I do think a love of the natural world creeps into my fiction. But it's something I do purely for myself and to share with others, unrelated to my career.

Can you share the inspiration or personal connection behind your novel "Michael Without Apology"?

I was mercilessly tormented as a child for perceived problems with my appearance. Nothing as dramatic as Michael's scars, but the abuse left scars of its own. I just turned 70, and ended up back in therapy trying to deal with a sort of post-traumatic stress from childhood bullying. I almost never know exactly where the stories come from, but I do know when my own life concerns cause me to choose a character with similar issues, and this is definitely one of those cases.

What is your process when transitioning between genres, such as fiction and nonfiction?

I'm actually quite bad at that, so I almost never do. I only have a couple (maybe three) nonfiction books, and none are recent.

How do you approach writing characters who face adversity and find redemption, like those in "Take Me

Catherine Ryan Hyde, the bestselling author whose timeless stories continue to resonate with readers around the world.

Catherine Ryan Hyde's profound storytelling, authentic characters, and compassionate themes solidify her as one of literature's most inspiring voices.

With You"?

I guess I'd say my approach is to try to write from that place where we are all human and all very much the same. In other words, under our differences is the basic experience of being alive. In that place, I'll understand what the character is feeling, and I trust that the reader will as well. Because we're all people.

Could you discuss your experiences working on the "Pay It Forward" movie adaptation and how it compared to writing the novel?

I had no involvement whatsoever with the adaptation. None. I did visit the set one day and met the actors, but I was not the screenwriter, nor was I any type of consultant. That arrangement is the usual one between authors and filmmakers.

How has aging and self-acceptance played a role in your writing process and themes?

I definitely know more about being happy as I get older. And anything I learn about myself and the world is going to end up in the mouth of one character or another. So I hope the books are going more deeply into the human experience as I myself do the same.

What lessons have you learned from your animal companions, and how have they made their way into your stories?

I've learned to talk less and listen more, even though we don't speak a common language. And I think the advantages to the work comes in the form of having animals characters who are each their own unique character. No generic golden retrievers whose job is simply to smile and hold up the other end of the leash.

Which of your books holds the most personal significance for you, and why?

I have a special place in my heart for a handful: Michael Without Apology; Have You Seen Luis Velez?; Boy Underground; So Long, Chester Wheeler; Life, Loss, and Puffins. I can't entirely say why. I just think they have the most to say about the world.

What advice would you give to aspiring authors struggling to find their voice or inspiration?

I would advise them to read. When you find the work you truly love to read, you'll be closer to what you want to write.

I hope the books are going more deeply into the human experience as I myself do the same.

Catherine Ryan Hyde

Lessons From A Literary Journey That Spans Decades

John Winn Miller's *Rescue Run* is a gripping sequel blending wartime thriller, espionage, and human resilience. Capt. Jake Rogers returns for a daring mission across Nazi-occupied Europe, facing tension-filled escapes, betrayals, and vivid foes like a ruthless bounty hunter. Richly detailed and deeply emotional, this historical saga delivers nonstop adventure and heart. Perfect for fans of action-packed wartime dramas!

John Winn Miller Shares Insights On His Award-Winning Historical Thrillers And The Art Of Storytelling

John Winn Miller discusses his journey from journalism to writing, the creative process behind his WWII historical novels, research challenges, character development, and his commitment to authenticity and emotional storytelling.

by Carine O'Leary

John Winn Miller is a master storyteller who has seamlessly transitioned from a distinguished career in journalism, screenwriting, and indie film production to crafting historical novels that balance razor-sharp authenticity with heart-pounding action. His debut novel, *The Hunt for the Peggy C*, captivated readers with its gripping World War II-era drama, earning awards and rave reviews for its blend of meticulous research and rich character development. Its sequel, *Rescue Run*, continues the saga with even greater stakes and emotional depth, drawing praise from literary giants like James Rollins for its "nonstop adventure" and riveting storytelling.

What sets Miller apart is his ability to bring history to life through unforgettable characters—like Captain Jake Rogers, a morally complex merchant sailor, and Miriam Maduro, a young Jewish woman turned fierce British intelligence agent—woven seamlessly alongside historical figures and real events. His cinematic writing style and exhaustive research create narratives that immerse readers in the brutal realities of World War II while celebrating courage against insurmountable odds.

In this exclusive interview, Miller shares the inspirations and challenges behind his work, offering insights into the meticulous craft of historical fiction. From his evolution as a writer to the delicate balance of action and character development, Miller's reflections inspire both readers and aspiring authors alike.

What inspired you to transition from journalism to writing historical fiction?

I wanted to be a novelist. But I realized I didn't know how to write. Plus, I had no exciting experiences to write about. Journalism seemed like the best way to remedy those deficiencies. After the newspaper industry collapsed in the early 2000s, I took a buyout and wrote screenplays. Then, when COVID hit, I decided to turn one of my screenplays into a novel. So why did I pick to write historical fiction about World War II? I didn't. It picked me after I watched a terrible movie years ago. I kept telling my family I could write a better screenplay. That night, I had a dream. When I awoke, I knew the first and last scenes and the name of the ship in my first novel, "The Hunt for the Peggy C," but nothing else. So, I had to spend the next few years filling in the cavernous gaps in my knowledge.

How did your experiences as a foreign correspondent influence your novels?

When I was traveling with Pope John Paul II, covering wars or reporting on terrorists' trials, there were no cell phones or internet. And CNN was in its infancy. As a result, I had to put the events in historical context and use all five senses in my reporting so readers would know exactly what happened and what it was like. They couldn't just Google it. That meant paying attention to even the smallest details, such as accents, clothing, scents, hand gestures, species of trees, types of vehicles, and types of weapons. That is very much my writing style now.

What is the research process like for creating such detailed and authentic historical settings in your books?

Books, books, books, documentaries, historical associations' websites, original documents online from the British National Archives, and even interviews conducted by the British Imperial War Museum with some of the real people in my books. I use footnotes to verify everything, and I hired experts to fact-check my work. One research problem was that I kept going down rabbit holes for hours in pursuit of one more interesting fact.

How do you balance thrilling action with deep character development in your storytelling?

It's a delicate balance. I have a propulsive writing style, sort of like watching a Bourne movie. At the same time, I have to slow down enough to make readers care about the characters. I try to do that with as little dialogue as possible, letting their actions and decisions under pressure reveal who they really are. At the same time, I sprinkle in bits of dialogue to disclose motivation and develop character arcs.

What motivated you to create the character of Capt. Jake Rogers, and how has he evolved across your novels?

Rogers is loosely based on America's first novelist, James Fenimore Cooper, who became a merchant sailor after being expelled from Yale for pulling pranks. My father was also kicked out of military school when he got in a fight standing up for what he thought was right. Rogers fled the US Naval Academy on a Europe-bound merchant ship while facing a possible murder charge for defending a friend in a fight. Like Rick in Casablanca, he begins as a cynical smuggler, indifferent to the war. But gradually, his sense of honor and love for Miriam Maduro make him realize that some things are worth fighting for.

Award-winning author John Winn Miller brings history to life through his acclaimed WWII novels, blending thrilling action and profound character development.

John Winn Miller masterfully blends historical precision, vivid storytelling, and emotional depth, crafting unforgettable narratives marked by courage and humanity.

Can you share any challenges you faced while writing "Rescue Run" and how you overcame them?

The novel was a constant challenge because I like to work my characters into a corner and then spend a considerable amount of time figuring out how they escape. That required a ton of research as I wanted everything to be both historically and technically accurate. So, the crazier their escapes seem, the more likely they are to be based on actual events. Also, I watched 1940s movies and listened to contemporaneous interviews to avoid using modern or incorrect phrases, particularly British ones ("knickers" instead of "underpants," for instance).

How did your experience as a screenwriter and producer shape your approach to novel writing?

Screenwriting is more like a haiku, sparse and focused on visuals. Bringing a script to life requires thorough research, meticulous planning, and a touch of ingenuity. My novels are like that. In fact, many reviewers say they are like watching a good action-adventure movie.

What were the most rewarding and most difficult aspects of writing about World War II-era Europe?

The most rewarding was bringing to life little-known, real-life heroes in the Dutch resistance, such as Jacoba van Tongeren (code-named Miss 2000), the only woman to create and lead a resistance movement. The horrible part was dealing with all the collaborators, bounty hunters, gangsters and indifferent people who willingly participated in the Nazi atrocities.

Who are your biggest writing influences, and how have they shaped your style?

I love non-fiction authors who write like novelists, such as Sebastian Junger (The Perfect Storm), as well as novelists who write with the authority of historians, like Colleen McCullough (Masters of Rome series). I try to emulate their mastery of detail but with a simpler, cinematic writing style. More Hemingway than Faulkner.

What advice would you give to aspiring authors looking to write historical fiction?

Pay attention to the little details and watch out for anachronisms.

"Historical fiction picked me after I watched a terrible movie and had a dream that inspired the first scenes of my novel."

John Winn Miller

Celebrating Stories Of Women Military Veterans

Sirrah Medeiros Explores The Dark Realms Of Reality And Imagination

Sirrah Medeiros discusses her award-winning books, anthologies, creative process, military influences, LGBTQ+ advocacy, and how her editorial expertise drives impactful horror, dark fantasy, and thriller narratives.

by Carine O'Leary

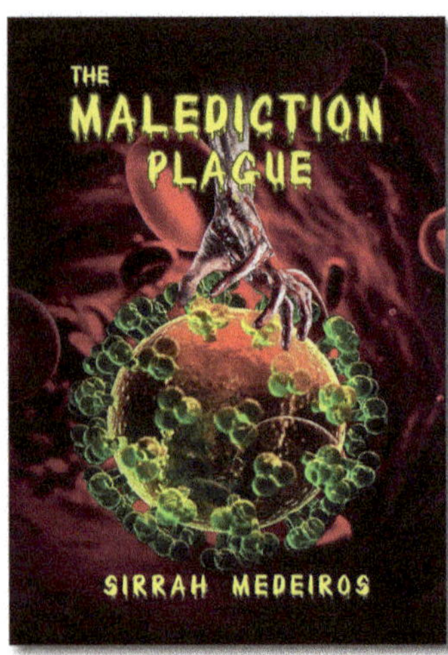

Sirrah Medeiros delivers a chilling masterpiece in *The Malediction Plague,* blending psychological complexity with gripping horror. Dr. Leon Fleischer's descent into madness and moral conflict unfolds against the backdrop of a catastrophic plague. Combining vivid storytelling with poignant themes of ego, guilt, and redemption, this novella is a haunting exploration of the human psyche. A must-read for fans of intelligent and unsettling horror.

Sirrah Medeiros stands as a beacon of storytelling brilliance, a masterful force in blending horror, dark fantasy, and thriller genres. An award-winning author, editor, anthologist, and Editor-in-Chief of Tundra Swan Press, Medeiros has carved a unique niche in the literary world, crafting tales that intertwine vivid imagination with profound emotional depth. With a steadfast dedication to her craft and an unyielding passion for advocacy, she weaves narratives that resonate with authenticity and explore the darkest corners of human experience.

As readers dive into "Secrets of Mother," the third entry in her award-winning Cristiane Bradford series, or the gripping standalone novella "The Malediction Plague," they encounter characters meticulously layered with complexity and nuance. Medeiros doesn't just write stories—she breathes life into her worlds, immersing readers in vivid landscapes fraught with suspense, horror, and humanity's inherent contradictions.

Beyond her own formidable creations, Medeiros champions diversity and inclusivity in literature. From highlighting voices of women military veterans in "The Haunted Zone" anthology to amplifying queer narratives in "Don't Ask, Ghosts Tell" alongside horror luminary Vince A. Liaguno, she brings fresh perspectives to the forefront, enriching genre fiction with vital and often underrepresented insights.

What solidifies Medeiros as not only a literary powerhouse but also an inspirational figure is how she channels her background—Marine Corps veteran, environmental management advocate, and LGBTQ+ ally—into her work. Her disciplined approach, combined with a profound understanding of humanity's trials and tribulations, allows her to create worlds that are both unsettling and deeply compelling.

In this exclusive interview, Sirrah Medeiros shares her journey as a storyteller, invaluable insights into her creative process, and thoughts on how her editorial acumen shapes her craft. Whether you're a devoted fan of her novels or an aspiring writer seeking wisdom, this conversation is certain to inspire, enthrall, and emphasize why Sirrah Medeiros belongs among the luminaries of contemporary fiction.

Secrets of Mother, the latest main entry in the Cristiane Bradford series, delves deeper into maternal themes. How did you develop Cristiane's emotional arc in this book?

Children sense when their parents aren't truthful, honest, or completely present. In relation to the character dynamics in Secrets of Mother, Cristiane's anxiety manifests because the relationship with her mother holds a secret at its core. That secret displayed in ways she could not understand—distance, conflict, and loneliness. Hiding a portion of herself, kept Beatrice from forming a foundational bond with Cristiane, and that lack of closeness grew into anxiety and insecurity which Cristiane carried throughout her high-school years, illustrated in the prequel, The Emerald Curse, and most of her college experience. Once the secret is resolved, both characters learn not only how to trust and interact together, but to grow as confident individuals.

The Malediction Plague is a standalone novella released in 2024. What unique narrative or thematic challenges did writing that plague-centered story present?

This story was fun to write. A thematic challenge I worked through was the psyche of the main character. He was raised by a father and grandfather who towed the line of nazi ideology. Yet, his mother was empathetic and cautioned him not to take the paternal creed at face value, but to question everything and reach his own conclusions. I had to research history in order to meld the egotistical, nazi-driven thinking with the scientist who is searching for an answer to a perceived problem. The character is ill-advised by his thoughts and internal dialog as he pursues a course of action any rational person would find abhorrent. Yet, as you follow the story, readers grasp that he has not lost his grip on morality all together. However, curiosity has a firm hold, which he indulges in horrific detail. Writing that character complexity was a challenge, but I believe it comes through to readers.

As editor of The Haunted Zone anthology, what criteria guided your selection of stories by women military veterans?

First, the authors had to be military veterans (or active duty) who identified as women. As the anthology was my first, and a passion project to highlight that demographic in the horror writing community, the initial criteria also narrowed the submission pool to a manageable level I could work through myself. Selection was based on the writer crafting a unique well-written story while remaining unified in tone to the overall theme. Selected stories reflect a vast array of haunting horrors from women's perspectives, such as loss, assault, war, trauma, and psychological horror.

You and Vince A. Liaguno are co-editing Don't Ask, Ghosts Tell. How is its focus different from The Haunted Zone, and what fresh voices are you highlighting?

Don't Ask, Ghosts Tell released in June 2025, my second anthology as an editor and publisher. Vince A. Liaguno's experience in the horror community as a writer, editor and anthologist was invaluable as we made our selections. Our focus was on the LGBTQ+ horror authors as book sales support the Modern Military Association of America, which provides assistance and advocacy to LGBTQ+ military members, veterans, and their families. The title is a play on the United States legislation Don't Ask, Don't Tell, that was repealed in 2011. However, the issue is relevant today, more so than expected when I mapped out the idea in 2023. We wanted the collection's focus to highlight the horrors and struggles people in the queer community may face or try to suppress depending on surroundings, societal pressure, and circumstances. Manifestations of grief, guilt, terror, PTSD, and other similar emotions are represented in the collection. Their stories' ghosts. Yet, truths always surface.

Along with many award-winning authors, we have amazing fresh voices in horror, such as May Walker, Amanda Nevade DeMel, and M. Edusa. Keep an eye on these newly published authors. They have much to offer.

Your background as a Marine Corps water purification specialist is unique. How has that shaped the realistic details or discipline in your horror and fantasy scenes?

My active military service was just over four years, but fueled a lasting interest in environmental and water quality issues that led to an environmental management degree. The structural foundation and discipline elevated by military service assisted in focus and drive throughout my life. However, it is the more than 25 years of education, travel, and life experiences—including a love of research and science, an inquisitive mind, and exposure to various cultures—that have profoundly influenced my writing, equipping me to create richly detailed fictional worlds.

As Editor-in-Chief at Tundra Swan Press, how does your editorial perspective feed back into your own writing process and world-building?

As an editor, I evaluate pacing, clarity, and emotional reckoning. That's made me more proficient in finding structural weaknesses early in my work. When I am worldbuilding, I focus on what details serve the story, rather than simply adding lore for lore's sake. I ask myself, would I accept this if someone submitted it to me? That question keeps my scenes focused and immersive rather than indulgent.

> Sirrah Medeiros captivates readers with her mesmerizing storytelling, creating deeply emotional, haunting tales that redefine horror and dark fantasy genres.

Being an editor has made me sensitive to what's missing—whether it's a gap in logic, emotional arc, or world rules. I use that skill when building my own fiction. I identify areas readers will instinctively question or want to explore further. Instead of patching over those gaps, I turn them into situations that pull readers deeper into the story.

Your works often bridge horror, dark fantasy, and thriller genres. How do you balance genre expectations while maintaining your distinct authorial voice?

Having a clear understanding of genres and subgenres is key to properly categorizing work and meeting reader expectations. My stories usually convey morals, virtue, or character growth amidst eerie settings, suspense, darkness, and persuasive characters. First, I write what interests me rather than following trends. Often, thrillers are a mainstream take on horror. As I steer toward crime thrillers, humanity's darkest and their victims, it's still horror. Dark fantasy simply involves weaving horror elements into the fantasy story arc, taking readers into or around the abyss as spells are cast and dragons slain.

What single piece of advice would you give aspiring authors, particularly those drawn to horror and dark fantasy fiction?

Write what makes you uncomfortable—what unsettles you. First, frighten yourself. Then, write it realistically onto the page. Your voice isn't going to appeal to everyone, but written authentically and with your own sense of genuine darkness, discomfort, or curiosity woven into the story, the reader will sense that and stay drawn to your work. A unique twist on age-old genre tropes is what will make your story stand out.

> *Write what makes you uncomfortable—what unsettles you. First, frighten yourself. Then, write it realistically onto the page.*
>
> **Sirrah Medeiros**

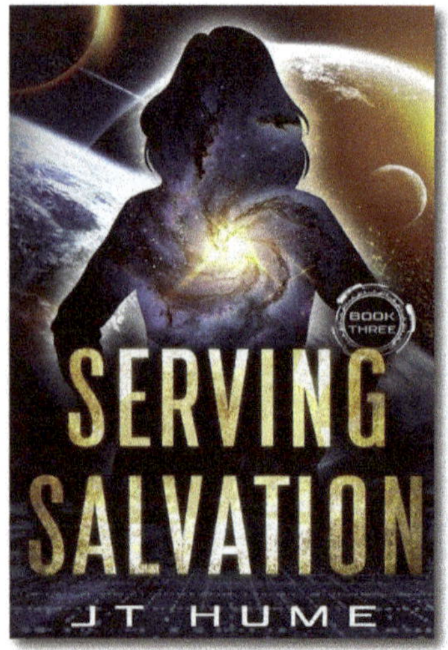

JT Hume Reflects On Writing, Life Experiences And Genre-Blending Mastery

JT Hume discusses his inspirations, multidimensional characters, and genre-blending craft, shaped by military service, Nevada's rugged terrain, and life lessons gleaned from love, chess, and collaboration.

JT Hume's *Serving Salvation: Book Three* is an exhilarating conclusion to a poignant sci-fi trilogy. With humanity's fate in the balance, the novel masterfully intertwines gripping political intrigue, thrilling mysteries, and unforgettable characters. From a sabotaged satellite to the haunting revelation of alien existence, each twist keeps readers on edge. Hume's skillful storytelling, coupled with layered human struggles, creates a thought-provoking space opera that is both heart-stirring and action-packed. A must-read for sci-fi enthusiasts!

By Novelist Post Staff

Few authors bring the richness of life's experiences into their storytelling quite like JT Hume. A gifted indie novelist and podcaster, Hume has cultivated a literary brand that defies easy categorization, weaving together elements of character-driven drama, gritty realism, and thought-provoking themes. Whether he's crafting a tale set against the stark, timeless backdrop of rural Nevada or transporting readers to the vast expanse of interstellar worlds, Hume's ability to blend genres—like romance, mystery, and politics—into seamless narratives is nothing short of impressive. His unique voice resonates, built on a foundation of personal triumphs, strategic depth, and the kind of genuine humanity we all crave in great fiction.

A Nevadan by choice and an Air Force veteran by service, JT Hume's life story reads like something out of his own novels, where resilience and adaptability shape the arcs of intriguing characters. His books have captivated readers for many reasons, but his ability to create multidimensional protagonists—such as Sheriff Maggie Doane in *A Sheriff in Nevada*—is a standout quality. His female leads are powerful yet nuanced, built from the examples of strong women he has encountered in his own life. Whether co-authoring with his wife, Cassidy Carson, or sculpting stories steeped in romance and redemption, Hume's works carry a deep sense of authenticity and heart, informed by over four decades of partnership with his soulmate.

In this exclusive interview, JT Hume takes us behind the curtain of his creative process, offering insights into his genre-spanning career, the influence of his Air Force service, and the undeniable impact of his personal life experiences. His thoughtful reflections and strategic genius, honed through years of playing chess and navigating the complexities of storytelling, showcase exactly why his novels resonate so deeply. Whether you're a fan of small-town mysteries or sweeping sci-fi romance epics, JT Hume promises stories that challenge, inspire, and entertain. Dive into this conversation and discover what makes this remarkable author one of the pillars of modern indie fiction.

What inspired you to write "A Sheriff in Nevada" and its sequel, "Downfall"?

I'm always intrigued by people-driven stories like "A Sheriff in Nevada." I published a series of books about Child Protective Services and became intrigued by the law enforcement side, but didn't want to write just another cop story. At the same time, I'm fascinated by rural Nevada, a vast area and culture almost frozen in time. How do I blend a modern crime story in an environment with gritty, memorable characters? And a tough-as-nails female lead character, to boot? The challenge helped me create my most popular books.

How do your experiences in the United States Air Force influence your storytelling?

The Air Force made me an author. Early in my enlistment, a senior leader discovered I could write, and he trusted me with a complex, high-visibility report for a critical project. Not long after, a short story I wrote was published in the University of Maryland's student fiction newsletter. Both were happy surprises that made me believe in myself as an author. Belief is powerful!

What draws you to writing about diverse settings, such as rural Nevada and interstellar journeys in the "Serving Salvation" series?

Nevada and space are remote and challenging environments, and they require strong personalities and hard decisions to survive. Layer the human condition on top of that, and you have the recipe for an engaging story where we read about characters who represent the best and worst of us, all struggling to survive.
My characters risk everything because they build in a better tomorrow. With this in mind, these settings lend themselves to excellent storytelling.

Can you share your writing process and how you balance genres like romance, politics, and mystery?

I'm the stepson of a professional violinist, and while I am not comparing myself to the classical greats, I understand how the blending of the numerous and diverse parts of an orchestra can produce a satisfying musical piece. Writing is the same, threading the complex elements of our humanity, society, and culture into a harmonious combination of literary fiction. I can only hope my stories are music for my readers' imaginations.

How do you go about creating complex, multidimensional characters like Maggie Doane in your novels?

I'm not afraid of borrowing examples from real life. Towards the end of my public service career, I was blessed to work with strong women whose leadership styles and personalities served as the role models for Sheriff Maggie Doane. Like Maggie, my supervisors were focused on solving problems and completing projects while balancing conflicting mission priorities and

Author JT Hume, turning life's journeys into unforgettable novels that redefine storytelling with heart, grit, and imagination.

troublesome personalities. Once I dropped my bosses into Maggie, the "Sheriff" books almost wrote themselves.

What challenges did you face when transitioning from one genre to another, such as from mystery to science fiction?

I feel the genre is not nearly as important as the people in the book. Like they say, "If you build it, they will come." If you write a good story with believable, heartfelt characters, then the genre becomes a living part of the adventure. The challenge for me after picking a genre is getting the essentials right, especially in science fiction. Respecting my readers' attention to detail helps keep them engaged in the story and makes for a better book.

How does your background in playing chess reflect in the strategic elements of your storytelling?

Chess is all about "Why did they make that move?" and "How do I react?". Your effectiveness as a player is your response to those questions, especially when calculating the most likely outcomes to the play on the board. It's the same with writers. Developing story elements based on those questions forces authors to develop plots around why a character acts as they do and how others in the book respond to that behavior. I'm not a great player, but I am a better writer because of chess.

What role does collaboration play in your work, particularly in co-authoring "From Tundra to Tiara"?

Collaboration is hard for me. I've spent a lifetime internalizing emotional events, and my writing sometimes reflects this. Co-writing FTTT with another author---who happened to be my wife---was outside my comfort zone, yet it evolved into what I feel is a natural progression in our relationship. The book became better because we did it together. The entire project made me more open to positive, constructive criticism and collaboration in general. It may not work for all writers, but for me, it was a humongous win-win.

How do your personal life experiences, like your long-lasting marriage, shape the romantic elements in your stories?

If any single life experience is in my books, it's the character arc towards becoming a better person. I was fortunate enough to marry the best person I will ever know, but doing so showed me where I needed to improve. This is a major plot point in "Love and Death on I-80 West," the graphic story about Tucci, the mass murderer slash ex-convict. He too met someone way above his level of emotional maturity, and he recognized he had to improve as a human being to be worthy of her. This non-traditional love story reflected my life lesson about romance: it's okay to be vulnerable to your soulmate will make you a better person.

What advice would you give to aspiring authors navigating the process of blending multiple genres effectively?

If you're asking about writers writing in multiple genres, the easiest advice is "Don't." Your literary life will be easier when you stick with a single genre. But humans can't do that. We are amazingly talented and complex. Even Robert Heinlein, the famous science fiction writer, said, "Specialization is for insects." When you cross genres or blend genres in a single book, do it because you have a story to tell and make sure that the genre you pick serves as characters in your story, not just as background. Your book will make for a much richer experience for your readers.

Friendship, Mystery, And Danger

Sophie McKenzie On Her Latest Murder Academy Series And The Art Of Writing Gripping Mysteries

The Sunday Times bestselling author Sophie McKenzie discusses her new Murder Academy series, the balance of suspense and sensitivity in teen mysteries, and advice for aspiring authors crafting compelling stories.

Sophie McKenzie's *Lessons in Death* is a thrilling start to the Murder Academy series, set in the eerie Mayfield Academy. When Georgia discovers her drama teacher's dead body in the library, only for it to vanish moments later, she's thrust into a gripping mystery. Joined by her best friend Billy and enigmatic newcomer Wren, Georgia faces danger and tests of loyalty as secrets unravel. Packed with suspense, sharp twists, and relatable teenage struggles, McKenzie combines intrigue with emotional depth. Perfect for fans of young adult mysteries and *Girl Missing*.

By Novelist Post Staff

Sophie McKenzie is, without question, one of the most dynamic voices in contemporary fiction. With a career spanning over three decades, her writing effortlessly cuts across genres and age groups, offering readers everything from heart-pounding thrillers to thoughtful reimaginings of beloved classics. Her ability to captivate audiences has made her a household name, not only as a Sunday Times bestselling author but also as a literary phenomenon whose books leave indelible marks on readers of all ages.

In this issue, we are ecstatic to present an exclusive interview with Sophie McKenzie as she unveils her latest venture into the world of teen murder mysteries: *Lessons in Death*, the first installment of the *Murder Academy* series. Sophie's knack for suspense shines brilliantly in this gripping tale, seamlessly blending adventure, humor, friendship, and the darker elements of mystery, all while maintaining age-appropriate sensitivity for younger audiences.

Sophie's novels are masterclasses in storytelling, and her passion for weaving intricate plots and dynamic characters is evident in every page she writes. From her award-winning teen thrillers like *Girl, Missing* to her compelling psychological dramas for adults such as *Trust in Me*, Sophie continues to redefine what it means to be a versatile author. And her commitment to accessibility, demonstrated in her dyslexia-friendly books, ensures that her stories resonate across barriers.

Join us as we dive into Sophie McKenzie's world—a world fueled by timeless passion for storytelling and a dedication to exploring the complexities of human relationships. In this candid interview, Sophie discusses friendship, trust, and suspense in her latest work, shares writing insights, and offers a sneak peek at what's next in the *Murder Academy* series. Whether you're a long-time fan or discovering her brilliance for the first time, Sophie McKenzie's work is an invitation you won't want to miss.

Please can you introduce your new book Lessons in Death?

Lessons in Death is a murder mystery set at Mayfield Academy (hence the series title, Murder Academy). The story begins when Georgia discovers one of her favourite teachers dead in the library. She rushes to get help, but when she returns a few minutes later, the body has disappeared. Georgia is certain a murder has taken place and that the person(s) responsible has moved the body, but only her best friend Billy believes her. Determined to work out what has happened and unmask the killer, the two of them hunt for evidence. But it isn't easy, especially when glamorous new girl Wren seems determined not only to get involved, but to get her hooks into Billy. With their friendship under strain and the investigation requiring more than a little rule-breaking, Georgia's stress levels quickly ramp up. And all that's before she realises that the killer knows what she's up to and is prepared to go to any lengths to stop her.

Can you talk about the role of friendship and trust in Lessons in Death?

Friendship is at the heart of the story. When the adult authorities (police, parents, teachers) refuse to believe Georgia has witnessed the aftermath of a murder, she feels very alone. Without her friends – and their trust in her – solving the mystery would be impossible.

It's always fun to explore the dynamics of any friendship group and how the separate and collective relationships work. For instance, who's the one with the practical know-how, who's the funny one, who's the one with the rebellious streak – and how do they all interact. Bringing Georgia and her friends together also allows for those lighter, more humorous touches which are a huge part of what I'm looking for myself when I'm reading a murder mystery.

What challenges did you face when writing a mystery for a younger audience?

The same challenges as with any book, for any audience! (Structuring a story, creating compelling characters, making what happens unexpected yet credible, etc etc.) The additional challenge of a murder mystery for a younger audience is in making sure there is plenty at stake, while handling murder/death/dead bodies in a sensitive and age-appropriate way.

How do you balance suspense and age-appropriate content in your teen thrillers?

For me, it's all in the specifics. There are certain things I avoid writing about. You won't find any blood or gore in my teen stories. Likewise, there's no swearing, graphically described violence or sexual content. Suspense isn't about the terrible thing, it's about the build up to it: the fear of discovery, the dangerous journey into the unknown and (to paraphrase Hitchcock) the knowledge that the bomb under the table will explode in fifteen minutes.

How does your approach differ when writing

Sophie McKenzie, the Sunday Times bestselling author of thirty novels, passionately shares her craft and unveils her latest mystery series, Murder Academy.

Sophie McKenzie's writing captivates readers with thrilling plots, relatable characters, and an unmatched ability to bridge audiences and genres.

for teens versus adults?

I don't really frame it from the outside in, like that. I start with the main character – what's their story and who might what to read it? – then work from there. I actually wrote my first adult thriller (Close My Eyes) because I had an idea that I knew that wouldn't be right for a teen audience; the character and their story dictate who the readers will most likely be.

Following on from that, one big difference in approach arises naturally from the main character's age. In adult books I'm most likely writing the thoughts, actions and speech of someone older and in teen books, the main characters are probably younger. Other than that, I'd say that my books for teens are usually shorter, so the plots are by definition less complicated – and I often find that my teen stories are more likely to revolve around the need to make morally thought-provoking choices while I'm also more careful around the handling of sensitive areas (like sex, violence and swearing). Finally, though I do love a dark, twisty ending, I would only ever close a book for teens on a note of hope.

Were any of the characters or settings in Lessons in Death inspired by real life?

No! I've tried writing characters from real life, and they don't really survive contact with the fictional story – the plot soon influences what they do, and they start to take on a life of their own. The only references to my own experience as a teenager are emotional, particularly Georgia's feelings of insecurity.

Do you plan for Lessons in Death to be part of a series, and what can readers expect next?

Yes! Lessons in Death is the first book in the Murder Academy series. Future stories will see Georgia and her friends solving more murder mysteries, both in and away from the school environment. The next story is set in a residential summer camp in the middle of nowhere, where Georgia and her friends investigate not one but two murders! Camp Murder is a fresh story, but hopefully featuring the same elements of danger, adventure, mystery, suspense, friendship and humour as book one.

What advice would you give to aspiring authors who want to write gripping mysteries for younger readers?

Read a lot and write a lot! The more you read (especially of the kind of thing you want to write) the more you'll absorb in terms of craft and technique. And the more you write, the more you are practising that craft and technique and developing your own story. It's important to break the journey up the huge mountain of an unwritten novel into a series of small steps, to stay open to making improvements and to remember that writing is mostly rewriting. Don't give up!

Finally, can you describe this new series in three words?

How about five:

Mystery. Suspense. Danger. Friendship. Fun.

Friendship is at the heart of the story.

Sophie McKenzie

Celebrating The Heartfelt Lessons And Whimsical Magic Of Tracy Watland's Writing

Tracy Watland Brings Positivity And Kindness To Life Through Stories That Inspire Children And Adults

Tracy Watland explores childhood creativity, emotional growth, and the power of kindness through her books, blending humor and heart to inspire children to embrace their voices and follow their dreams.

by Carine O'Leary

Tracy Watland's books are a delightful blend of humor, heart, and inspiration. Her stories encourage kindness, self-belief, and emotional growth, captivating young readers with relatable characters and whimsical adventures. From embracing individuality to fostering compassion, her imaginative tales carry empowering lessons that resonate deeply. Perfect for children, parents, and educators alike, Tracy's work is a celebration of positivity and creativity.

Tracy Watland is a treasure in the world of children's literature—a writer who doesn't just pen stories, but crafts whole worlds infused with humor, heart, and hope. Her books are not mere tales; they are guiding lights, illuminating paths of kindness, courage, and self-belief for young minds. Whether it's through the whimsical verses of *The Witch's New Britches*, the empowering lessons of *Bluebird of Happy*, or the magical musical adventures found in *Abby's Magic Music: Billy's Story*, Tracy's work resonates deeply and meaningfully with children and adults alike.

As a Kindness Advocate and a relentless pursuer of positivity, Tracy has mastered the art of weaving life-changing emotional lessons into her stories with remarkable ease. Her natural ability to connect with children—through humor, vulnerability, and wisdom—ensures her books are not only entertaining but transformative. And it's not just young readers who find solace in her words; parents and educators cherish Tracy's works for the lasting impact they create.

In this upcoming interview, we had the incredible opportunity to delve into the mind of this luminous author. Tracy shares the motivation behind her uplifting stories, the influences from her own childhood, and the remarkable moments where her work sparked movements of kindness and connection. Fueled by creativity and love, Tracy Watland's books are a testament to the belief that every child's voice matters, and every act of kindness has the potential to ripple into something extraordinary. Prepare to be inspired by the magic she creates, one story at a time.

What inspired you to start writing children's books centered on positivity and self-belief?

A child's mind is most open and receptive during the first 7 years. This is when fundamental beliefs, behaviors and habits that can impact someone's lives are developed. I wanted to share happy messages to reinforce that foundation for kids; helping them grow into kind, secure grown-ups.

How did your own childhood experiences influence the themes in your stories?

Louise Hay from Hay House Publishing once told me to write books that I needed as a child, and to write what I would've wanted to read as a kid. So, I took all the things I loved -giving, helping, animals, music, etc. and created a world I'd want to live in through my books.

Can you share the story behind The Witch's New Britches and what message you hoped to convey through it?

That was a silly poem that popped into my head when I was driving home from a "Writing for Children" class I took at Columbia College in Chicago years ago. It was also written for my Godchildren. It's meant to make kids laugh with a subtle message that it doesn't matter how the world sees you. It's about what you have underneath it all that counts.

The Kindness Can encourages compassion and courage—how did you come up with the "rules" in the book?

I wanted to write about what Kindness can do. And I love doing Random Acts of Kindness..or being a RAKer. As I was researching other stories about Kindness there were so many conflicting messages about what being kind means. I wanted it to be simple, because it is. Be Compassionate, Be Courageous, simply Decide and do it. I wanted to collect all those Kind acts somewhere others could see and be inspired to do their own. So all the things Kindness can do evolved into The Kindness Can. Currently out of print but coming back in 2026 to celebrate its 10th Anniversary.

What role does music play in Abby's Magic Music: Billy's Story, and why did you choose it as a central theme?

I'm a music lover. Music makes EVERYTHING better. I have a lot of friends who are musicians, and one particular friend owns a musical instrument store that is truly pure Magic. It's the perfect setting to tell many character-building stories through many musical characters; some of whom actually hang out in the real store.

In Bluebird of Happy, Mac overcomes criticism to find his voice—how important is this lesson for children today?

It's crucial! There are so many loud and/or bullying voices that get heard simply because of the volume of delivery. Sometimes the more gentle or quiet voices are drowned out. I was one of those kids whose voice was often overpowered by more forceful opinions. I often felt what I had to say didn't matter. Or I wasn't being heard. Life finally taught me that everyone's voice counts, and people don't have to agree with you. But whatever your gift is, you are meant to share it. And whatever you feel you want to give a voice to; you should speak it. The right people will hear you. And it might be exactly what they need to hear too.

How do you balance humor and deeper emotional messages in your books for young readers?

By making it a safe space. Humor is the way into kids'

PHOTO: Tracy Watland, Author Of Heartwarming And Empowering Children's Stories, Advocates For Kindness And Positivity With Her Signature Creativity And Enthusiasm.

Tracy Watland's transformative stories champion kindness, courage, and self-belief, leaving lasting impact on young hearts and growing minds.

hearts and minds. It creates safety, making them feel more engaged and open. I use humor to build connection, but I also make sure there's room for real emotion underneath the laughs; along with a character to help guide them through the tricky or scary parts. I want kids to feel seen and empowered when they finish my books. I feel like humor keeps things light enough to carry some of the heavier emotions. And I make sure to give them tools to work through it all.

What has been the most touching response you've received from a parent or child about your work?

There are so many, but it truly touches my heart when a parent thanks me for writing a particular book because the message is exactly what their child needed to hear. Or when a child wants to share a secret or story with me related to one of my characters, because they know I'm a safe space and I understand them. I think my favorite moment was when a school built their own giant Kindness Can and used it to collect food donations for a local food pantry. They were so proud to show it to me during my visit, and I was so proud of them for taking Kindness and The Kindness Can to another level.

Do you have a particular writing routine or ritual that helps you tap into your creativity?

Not really. I've always been a "just wing it", ride the wave when it hits you kinda girl. I know who my characters are, and I know what my message is. I also know where I want to start and where I want to finish each book. I leave it up to my characters to tell me their story. And sometimes I edit and re edit until it's just right. Sometimes they tell me when I'm driving or in the shower or taking care of my flowers. Sometimes I get "messages" in song lyrics. Sometimes they wake me up at 3am. When the time is right it just flows through me.

What advice would you give to aspiring children's authors who want to write with heart and purpose?

Follow your heart. Write the stories your 5 year old or 10 year old self wanted to read. And don't worry so much about all the "rules." Somehow, some way, your story/book will end up where it's supposed to be in the hands of who needs it. If you have an idea or a desire to write it's because you're the one that's meant to bring that story into the world. NEVER give up!

> *A child's mind is most open and receptive during the first 7 years.*
>
> **Tracy Watland**

Exploring the Life and Works of a Literary Sensation

GREGG HURWITZ

Leads the Charge in the Art of Creative Storytelling

by Carine O'Leary | London

Gregg Hurwitz discusses the evolution of his iconic Orphan X series, his dynamic career across creative mediums, and his thought-provoking efforts to bridge political and cultural divides.

Gregg Hurwitz is a tour de force in the world of storytelling, a master craftsman whose stories have enthralled millions of readers and viewers across the globe. With a literary repertoire that spans 24 internationally bestselling thrillers, including the captivating *Orphan X*series, Gregg's work has become synonymous with pulse-pounding action, complex characters, and narratives that delve deep into the human psyche. His ability to weave high-stakes drama with heart-stirring emotional depth is unparalleled, earning him a place on the New York Times bestsellers list and the hearts of thriller enthusiasts in over 33 languages worldwide.

But to label Gregg Hurwitz as merely an exceptional novelist would be an incomplete portrait of his artistry. This is a storyteller who has left an indelible mark on every medium he has touched, from film and television to comic books and poetry. His contributions to iconic franchises like *Batman*and *Wolverine*show his flair for breathing new life into beloved characters, while his original creations, such as the indomitable Evan Smoak, reveal his ability to craft heroes that resonate deeply with readers long after the final page is turned. It takes a rare gift to blend cerebral depth with explosive action, and Gregg does so with unerring precision, keeping us transfixed and on the edge of our seats.

Beyond the brilliance of his fictional creations, Gregg is a thoughtful observer of the human condition. His exploration of themes such as justice, vengeance, and moral ambiguity speaks to his nuanced understanding of the world, while his efforts against growing polarization in politics and culture highlight his courage and conviction. Gregg is not only one of the most prolific and versatile authors of our time, but also a voice of empathy and reason in an era that sorely needs it.

It was a true privilege to sit down with Gregg Hurwitz for this issue of *Novelist Post*. In this candid conversation, Gregg opens up about his creative process, his dynamic career, and the inspiration behind the unforgettable characters and stories that have earned him his rightful place as a giant in modern literature. Whether you're a longtime fan of Gregg's work or new to his page-turning adventures, this interview offers insights into the mind of a storyteller whose words continue to leave an indelible mark on readers worldwide.

Your career spans across novels, screenplays, comics, and even poetry. How do you approach writing for these different mediums, and how does each format influence your storytelling techniques?

Answer: I like to put my head down and blast on one project. Then move to the next and do the same. I don't do as well working on one thing in the morning and something else in the afternoon. But sometimes when deadlines crowd in on me I'm forced to do that. It takes a lot of focus.

Novels are quite different from, say, screenplays. Books are 400 pages of final product. A script is

Continued *on page 34*

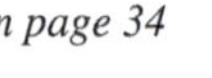

"Gregg Hurwitz: The Mastermind Behind The Orphan X Series And A Visionary Storyteller Of Our Time.

Photo by Gary Fleder

Continued *from page 32*

110 pages with a lot of white on the page—and they are recipes for a creative work, not the creative work itself. One way to think of a script is as an invitation to collaborate.

The Orphan X series has captivated readers with its intense action and complex protagonist, Evan Smoak. What inspired you to create this character, and how has he evolved over the course of the series?

Orphan X is the culmination of decades of writing and research. It took a lotta years for me to find my way to Evan. And fair enough. He's a hard guy to find. He was yanked out of a foster home at the age of twelve, raised in a covert black assassin program buried so deep within the U.S. government that virtually no one knows it exists. And I didn't want this to feel like nonsense Hollywood training, you know, where he's catching flies with chopsticks. All in an effort to show the process by which a skinny, scared kid from an East Baltimore boy's home could plausibly transform into Orphan X, a legendary figure in the shadow service. The idea of him derived from my friends who have worked in black ops. I wondered about a program that would take young foster kids, kids no one wanted, that would raise them to be in essence expendable weapons. I wove facts into fiction, all the while concentrating on who my character would be. Once I had a handle on Evan Smoak, I knew that this adventure would follow. And many more.

One of my favorite things about writing Evan Smoak is the way he's evolved and changed across the stories. When he was first taken out of the foster home, his handler and father figure told him, "The hard part isn't turning you into a killer. The hard part is keeping you human." As much as the Orphan X books are a thriller series, they're also about Evan's process of learning what it means to be human.

You've done extensive research for your thrillers, including sneaking onto demolition ranges with Navy SEALs and going undercover into mind-control cults. Can you share a favorite experience?

Probably when I was with my dear friend Billy Stojack (RIP), who I based the character of Tommy after. We were out at his Vegas ranch hanging out, looking through his gear, and he gave me his big goofy grin, hefted a rocket-propelled grenade launcher, and said, "Wanna go out in the desert and play adult lawn darts?"

In addition to writing fiction, you've been actively working against polarization in politics and culture. How do you see your role as an author and public figure contributing to this cause, and what impact do you hope to achieve?

Part of why I'm effective—to whatever extent I am—is that I'm not a political pundit. Being a novelist taught me to burrow deep into different perspectives. When I'm writing a character, I'm trying to pull on the mask of their experience and see the world through their eye holes. When people approach those they disagree with politically or culturally, they are usually trying to prove them wrong. I'm not. I'm approaching with curiosity to see what I might learn.

Your novels often explore themes of justice, vengeance, and moral ambiguity, as seen in The Kill Clause and The Survivor. How do you navigate these complex themes, and what message do you hope to convey to your readers through your stories?

I don't think of it like this, at least not consciously when I'm writing. All I'm thinking about is character and story. But I suppose what my stories illustrate is how to navigate a world of threat, chaos, and constant change while not compromising one's ethics. How to hold meaning even in the face of great threat and fear. And how the grace and grit of a single individual can change the world.

You've written for iconic comic book characters like Batman and Wolverine. How does writing for established characters in a shared universe differ from creating your own characters and worlds, and what unique challenges and rewards come with each?

Well, there are certainly more limitations. With my books and original screenplays, I can have my characters do anything I wish. But when I'm writing, say, Batman or Punisher, there are constraints around them as a brand. Batman's been around since before I was born and he'll be around long after I'm dead. So I view those jobs as holding a public trust in a way. I want my own mark and creativity to be left on the stories I write and I hope to texture the characters in ways that are new and revelatory but I do not own them. They are not mine. They are the best, best toys that the rich neighbor who lives up the street lets me play with. And I'm grateful to have the chance to do so.

Gregg Hurwitz is a literary powerhouse whose storytelling brilliance has captivated global readers with unforgettable characters and thrilling adventures.

> *"Gregg Hurwitz might very well be the best action-thriller writer of our time"*
> **— Booktrib**

> *"This is the perfect place to start for newcomers to the series, while fans will eagerly want to see what happens next. Hurwitz and his antihero get better with each book."*
> **— Jeff Ayers,** FirstClue

> *"Replete with all of your favorite characters, and a handful of side quests, Antihero may be one of the best books I've read in a long time."*
> **— Stuart Ashenbrenner,** Best Thriller Books

> *"Awesome and propulsive—Big Bourne and Reacher energy."*
> **— The New York Times**

> *"One of the best thrillers around. You won't put this one down."*
> **— The Globe and Mail**

> *"A crushingly brilliant piece of fiction."*
> **— Best Thriller Books**

GREGG HURWITZ

Gregg Hurwitz is the New York Times, #1 internationally bestselling author of 24 thrillers, including the Orphan X series, and two award-winning thriller novels for teens. His novels have won numerous literary awards, graced top ten lists, and have been published in 33 languages. Gregg currently serves as the Co-President of International Thriller Writers (ITW).

Gregg has written screenplays for or sold spec scripts to many of the major studios (including SWEET GIRL and THE BOOK OF HENRY), and written, developed, and produced television for various networks. He is also a New York Timesbestselling comic book writer, having penned stories for AWA (Knighted and the critically acclaimed anthology NewThink), Marvel (Wolverine, Punisher) and DC (Batman, Penguin). He has published poetry, numerous academic articles on Shakespeare, taught fiction writing in the USC English Department, and guest lectured for UCLA, and for Harvard in the United States and internationally. In 2022, he helped write the opening ceremony of the World Cup. In the course of researching his thrillers, he has sneaked onto demolition ranges with Navy SEALs, swum with sharks in the Galápagos, and gone undercover into mind-control cults.

Currently, Gregg is actively working against polarization in politics and culture. To that end, he's produced several hundred commercials and creative content which have gotten several hundred million views on digital TV platforms. His editorial pieces have appeared in The Wall Street Journal, The Guardian, The Huffington Post, The Bulwark, The Telegraph, Salon,and others.

Explosive Action Meets Emotional Depth: A Gripping Addition to the Orphan X Series

Intense, action-packed, and otionally gripping, Nemesis showcases Gregg Hurwitz's unparalleled storytelling, aving readers captivated till the final page.

Gregg Hurwitz delivers another relentless and adrenaline-pumping thriller in *Nemesis*, the tenth installment in the Orphan X series. This book cements the series' reputation as a masterclass in modern action storytelling, blending high-stakes drama, morally complex characters, and sharp tactical precision that keeps readers on the edge of their seats.

Evan Smoak, the enigmatic and deadly Orphan X, finds himself in a deeply personal conflict when he's betrayed by Tommy Stojack, his trusted gunsmith and loyal confidant. The betrayal hits deeply, forcing Evan to confront his rigid code of ethics while plotting his retaliation. Hurwitz skillfully crafts scenes filled with pulse-pounding action, vivid fight sequences, and psychological tension as Evan faces challenges not just from his enemies, but also within himself.

What sets *Nemes is* apart is Hurwitz's ability to interweave action with humanity. Amid the relentless pace, moments of humor and emotional depth allow readers to connect with Evan beyond his assassin persona. The betrayal by Stojack also pushes Evan into uncharted territories, showing the rare vulnerabilities of a hardened operator.

Though the pacing fluctuates in quieter sections, these moments serve to deepen the story's complexity, laying a strong foundation for the explosive finale. Hurwitz expertly balances brutal combat with thought-provoking moral quandaries, making *Nemesis*an unputdownable addition to the series.

For fans of thrillers, *Nemesis*proves why the Orphan X series continues to lead its genre. Action-packed, emotionally resonant, and brilliantly executed, this is Gregg Hurwitz at his absolute best. 4.5/5 stars.

Anthony Bidulka Reflects on Crafting Stories of Diversity and Connection

by Carine O'Leary

Award-Winning Author Telling Unique Stories With Heart, Humor, And Mystery

Anthony Bidulka illuminates rural life, identity, and resilience through his award-winning crime fiction, featuring diverse characters and gripping mysteries that challenge conventions while reflecting his philanthropic philosophy and deep personal passion.

Anthony Bidulka's literary journey is one forged with passion, introspection, and a deep connection to the human experience. From the wide-open, picturesque prairies of Saskatchewan to the layered complexities of diverse, underrepresented characters, his work explores themes of identity, belonging, and resilience. Bidulka's stories are rooted in tradition but branch into fresh, uncharted territories, challenging the norms of genre fiction while staying grounded in powerful, accessible storytelling.

With accolades such as the Crime Writers of Canada Award of Excellence and the Lambda Literary Award, Bidulka has solidified his place as an influential voice in contemporary crime fiction. Yet his work goes far beyond plots and puzzles. Novels such as Going to Beautiful provide windows into lives and locations often overlooked, casting light on what it means to live authentically while wrestling with profound loss, self-discovery, and human connection. His ability to balance humor, tenderness, and thrilling suspense is a testament to his gift as a storyteller and his commitment to creating nuanced, richly human tales.

Anthony Bidulka's writing serves as both an escape and a call to reflect—to see the world and ourselves more completely. Whether through the first-of-its-kind adventures of his transgender private investigator Merry Bell or the culturally resonant narratives of his standalone novels, Bidulka challenges readers to expand their view of what is possible in literature and in life. His stories do more than entertain; they amplify voices, touch hearts, and remind us all of the extraordinary within the ordinary.

Photo: *Anthony Bidulka, award-winning author whose work celebrates diversity while captivating readers with humor and suspense. Credit: David Stobbe*

What inspired you to leave your career as a professional accountant to pursue writing full-time?

Writing has been a passion of mine for as long as I can remember. Growing up on a farm in rural Saskatchewan I had no role models, I didn't know a single writer, writing was more a dream than career option. I went on to receive three degrees from the University of Saskatchewan. After earning my Certified Professional Accountant (CPA) designation I moved on to a career as a corporate auditor with the firm of Ernst & Young. I was ten years into that career and reaching one of those milestone ages, when it struck me that if I was ever to take a chance to pursue my passion and try my hand at writing, this was the time. I had a good career to fall back on and a supportive spouse and family. These were my safety nets. So I leapt. I left my job at E&Y and delved fulltime into writing. That was twenty-five years ago. Fortunately, things turned out for me.

How did your Saskatchewan roots influence the settings and themes of your novels?

Inspecting my body of work it's easy to see my rural Saskatchewan roots significantly influencing my writing. Growing up when and where I did, there wasn't a great deal of opportunity to know the world and figure out if there was a place in it for someone like me. Life was small and restrictive yet bucolic and beautiful and I struggled between wanting to never leave and knowing I needed to. That struggle and tension, along with plenty of love and appreciation for the prairie life, are evident in most of my books.

What inspired Russell Quant's character, and why did you choose to make him a private detective?

Being very aware that I was entering into a very competitive career path, I thought a lot about how to distinguish myself amongst the multitude of writers I saw represented on the shelves of libraries and bookstores. I was also coming to an awareness that with the privilege of being a writer comes an opportunity to present to the world something worthwhile and important. I was just coming to define myself as a writer and why I wanted to write. It took me a while, but today I know my WHY. It is this: I write to tell stories of underrepresented people and underrepresented places in a way that is accessible and, hopefully, entertaining. Russell Quant answered that WHY perfectly.

Could you share any behind-the-scenes challenges you faced while writing your award-winning book "Going to Beautiful"?

An unexpected challenge was responding to an editor's concern regarding a scene that involved a murder in a religious, educational, Saskatchewan setting. It was an apt concern because at the time the news was full of stories relating to the discovery of unmarked gravesites at residential schools. Although my story had no relation to these horrific events, my editor rightly pointed out that we needed to consider changing the scene, removing it altogether or directly addressing the issue in the story. We chose the latter.

> Bidulka is a masterful storyteller blending humor, suspense, and authenticity, amplifying underrepresented voices while redefining the boundaries of crime fiction.

What do you think makes the Merry Bell series unique among contemporary crime mysteries?

As far as the Canadian crime writing genre goes, I believe Merry Bell is the first and only kick-butt, transgender PI hanging out her shingle in a small prairie city. A recent book reviewer said: "These books aren't just about a case or a mystery to be solved, they are explorations into human beings and relationships...". I think this too speaks to what is special about the Merry Bell series.

How do you approach writing diverse and underrepresented characters with authenticity and relatability?

I take this very seriously. The key, I feel, is taking the time to ensure that I can represent these characters with as much awareness, understanding and respect as possible. My process is not just creating characters, it's writing about people. If I don't feel confident about a specific character, I put in the work until I do, or conclude that I don't (at least not yet) and do not proceed.

What was your reaction to being the first Canadian to win the Lambda Literary Award for Best Men's Mystery?

Aside from yipping and hollering like I was the first person to land on the moon? I was surprised, grateful, humbled and excited all at the same time, especially to have it happen so early in my career (my second book). Winning an award is personally rewarding, but I knew even then, as I do now, that it also comes with opportunity. The opportunity arises with increased exposure and public awareness of your work. Especially for a writer like me, writing the books I do, there is unmatched opportunity to serve my WHY, to expand the representation of the people and places I feel are currently underrepresented in crime fiction.

Can you describe how your philanthropic efforts and community work have impacted your writing or storytelling?

From my perspective, philanthropy, community and volunteer work, all of it is undertaken with similar, parallel goals: the hope that what you contribute might help to make the world a little better than how you found it. In a way, my books are mirrors of this philosophy, presenting a fictional world that is perhaps a little better than it really is, as an inspiration for how it can be.

How do you balance humor, tenderness, and suspense in your mystery novels?

Perhaps one of my weaknesses as a crime writer is that I am often waylaid by the human stories I wish to tell. I write mysteries. Without balance, you risk losing the interest of readers who come to your work for that specific reason. To keep myself in check, at the beginning of each project I create two outlines. One focuses on the crime and "whodunit", the other on character arcs. In combining the two I find the balance that serves both.

What advice would you give to aspiring authors who want to explore unconventional or underrepresented narratives in their work?

The first thing I suggest any writer do is ask themselves one question: Why do I write? Believe me, the question is not easy to answer, and the answer can change as we grow and develop. Do you want to entertain? Educate? Convince? Challenge? Armed with your answer, one you can stand by and believe in, will help you immensely as you build a career, transform ideas into written words and convince others to read them. If your why encompasses exploring unconventional and underrepresented narratives, then ask yourself the next questions: Why you? Why are you the best person to tell these stories? What contribution can you make?

Find your why, then find your way.

Anthony Bidulka's *Home Fires Burn* masterfully blends gripping mystery, emotional depth, and poignant themes of identity and family. Merry Bell's investigation into a chilling death uncovers hidden truths while confronting her own past. A compelling finale to the trilogy, Bidulka delivers suspense and heart in equal measure. Highly recommended for crime fans!

Experiences inform beliefs and responses, so the narrative of my client's life tells me a lot about their struggles."

Donna E. Lane

Donna E. Lane Shares Her Deeply Moving Stories Of Faith, Healing And Redemption

By Novelist Post Staff

Photo: *Dr. Donna E. Lane and her husband, David, share a serene, reflective moment together, embodying the partnership and inspiration behind her transformative storytelling and faith-centered works.*

Fiction Rooted In Spiritual And Psychological Truths

Dr. Donna E. Lane discusses her unique approach to storytelling, blending spiritual depth, psychological insights, and personal experience to create powerful faith-based novels and transformative devotionals across multiple genres.

Dr. Donna E. Lane stands as a beacon of literary excellence, seamlessly blending her expertise as a Christian counselor and spiritual director with her profound gift for storytelling. Her works not only entertain but deeply challenge and inspire, inviting readers to grapple with themes like trauma, faith, redemption, and the complexities of human relationships. Through her meticulously crafted characters and riveting narratives, she offers both solace and wisdom that transcend the pages of her books. Whether she's guiding readers through Biblical reflections, exploring frontier life, or revealing fantastical worlds, Dr. Lane's voice resounds with authenticity and purpose.

Her ability to weave spirituality and psychological depth into her stories is nothing short of remarkable. Books like *This Hallowed Ground* and *Scorched Earth* transport readers to emotionally staggering moments in history, while her devotional works—*The Way of the Shepherd*, *Dwelling*, and *Seeking Treasures*—offer invaluable spiritual reflection forged from her own life's trials and triumphs, including the poignant loss of her son, Cody. Courageous, heartfelt, and deeply rooted in faith, Dr. Lane delivers narratives that resonate with profound truth and hope.

In this exclusive interview, Dr. Donna E. Lane takes us behind the scenes of her extraordinary writing process, shares the motivations that fuel her work, and offers insights from her personal and professional journey. Prepare to be captivated by an author whose words not only tell stories but transform hearts. It is a privilege to showcase her voice in this issue of *Novelist Post* —a voice that continues to enrich lives and elevate the literary world.

Your historical novel, This Hallowed Ground, vividly portrays frontier life—how did your experience as a Christian counselor influence your depiction of the challenges your characters face?

My first step in writing any novel involves fleshing out the main characters by building an extensive backstory, most of which will never make it into the novel. For the main character in This Hallowed Ground, Mac, I imagined his parents' and grandparents' history and beliefs, which directly impacted Mac's development. I learned about this process from my experience as a Christian counselor, where one of the first things I do is ask the client to share their life story—childhood experiences and relationships, the nature of their parents' marriage, extended family history, and any significant events or traumas in their lives. Experiences inform beliefs and responses, so the narrative of my client's life tells me a lot about what their struggles will be in the present. In the same way, the "experiences" of my main characters inform how they view and respond to their world. This process also helps make my characters multidimensional and realistic, helping readers to relate to them as individuals, even if their experiences are vastly different, such as living through the Civil War and the Western frontier.

What motivations prompted you to write This Hallowed Ground and Scorched Earth?

My husband and I took a summer trip out west to canyon country, and during that trip,

> Dr. Donna E. Lane masterfully weaves spiritual truths with compelling narratives that enrich lives and challenge readers to embrace healing and hope.

we drove through the Navajo reservation. I was moved to tears by the experience. They've been relegated to land that settlers deemed useless, with little or no means to provide for themselves, leaving them dependent on a government that cares little for their fate. For strong, proud people, the psychological consequences of this mistreatment would be enormous. I was also struck by how little notice, comparatively, is given to their story and the horrors that led to where they are now. I told my husband if I were starting my career instead of moving toward retirement, I would move out west and counsel the indigenous population. He suggested I write their story instead.

In Scorched Earth, redemption is a central theme. How did you balance portraying hardship and faith without tipping into sentimentality?

I anchored this series in the story of Job as its Scriptural foundation. Job's story doesn't tend toward sentimentality, but it speaks about the kind of deep faith that sustains someone through significant trauma and loss. I don't "sugarcoat" the pain with a whitewash of faith in these stories; instead, I explore how faith can promote posttraumatic growth, which research shows is beneficial in healing from significant pain and suffering. Finding the redemption in a trauma narrative is part of posttraumatic growth.

The Way of the Shepherd, Dwelling, and Seeking Treasures offer spiritual reflections—how did your personal spiritual journey shape its devotional tone?

My youngest son, Cody, had a progressive neurological disorder, resulting in his death at age 17. His life journey, his relationship with Christ, and his loss have had a significant impact on my spiritual journey. I've said many times, if I didn't have Jesus to carry me through the most terrifying, powerless, and overwhelming experience of my life, I would've curled up in the fetal position and never moved again. Cody taught me more than anyone else in my life about how to walk through suffering and face death, about what it means to have a true connection with Jesus, and about the strength God provides through faith. I share the lessons I learned from him in my devotional and Biblical study books.

Your background in counseling informs complex character motivations—can you share a scene where that insight surprised even you?

In This Hallowed Ground, Mac returns from the Civil War to find his mother and sisters murdered by Union soldiers in his absence. Writing the unfolding of the scene where he learned of their fate and his responses to their loss was a deeply emotional experience for me, and I was surprised by the turn it took. Mac had faced unbelievable trauma during the war, from being wounded to seeing his father and best friend killed to being forced to kill opposing soldiers against his religious beliefs. Yet, it was the loss of his family that broke him. In a last-ditch effort to reclaim his family's stolen land, Mac traded five years of his life to the Union army—the very people who committed those heinous murders—to fight the natives in the west in exchange for his land.

In The Interview, choices and consequences drive the narrative—what personal or professional experiences shaped that theme?

The importance of choices and the acceptance of responsibility for those choices and their consequences is a major theme in my Christian counseling and spiritual direction practice. I work primarily with trauma survivors, so I'm well-acquainted with the victim mentality that can come from experiencing abuse and other forms of trauma. Survivors often feel a loss of authority over their lives, and in fact, it was true that they didn't choose their traumatic experiences. But when that victimized thinking extends forward from the trauma into the rest of their lives, the damage done by the abuser or trauma experience continues as if the trauma is still happening in their present. The result is extremely damaging emotionally and psychologically. The Interview explores the choices of one young trauma survivor as she faces the temptations of evil and her own demons during an interview with Satan.

You draw inspiration from Tolkien and Lewis—how have their works influenced your world building and theological themes?

I admire Lewis' brilliance in explaining Biblical truths in unique ways that challenge and enlighten. He crossed over genres, which encouraged me to write in multiple genres, despite all the feedback I received urging against it. Tolkien is the grandfather of fantasy fiction. He has no equal. His use of theological themes without preaching or heavy-fisted allegory is something I aspire to mirror. The Interview is based on Lewis' Screwtape Letters, my fantasy series mirrors many elements of Lewis' Space Trilogy, and Dwelling explores the same concepts as Lewis' Great Divorce.

What one piece of practical advice would you offer aspiring authors aiming to write compelling, faith based fiction?

Write what is in your heart.

> *Scorched Earth* masterfully intertwines raw human struggle with Western grandeur, delivering an emotionally charged epic. Mac and Ester's gripping journey through adversity and love captivates, highlighting resilience against the unforgiving backdrop of the American West. A multi-award-winning triumph that promises depth, drama, and an unforgettable tale of redemption and survival.

> *Experiences inform beliefs and responses, so the narrative of my client's life tells me a lot about their struggles."*
>
> **Donna E. Lane**

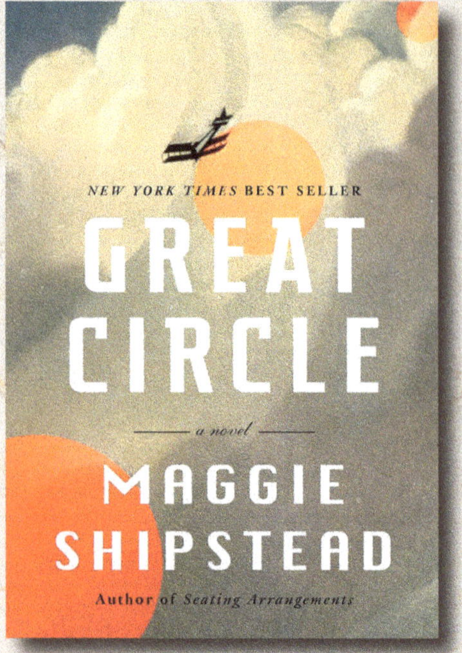

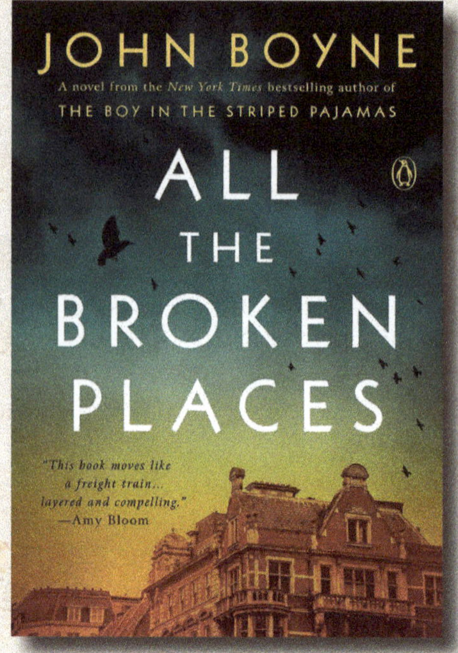

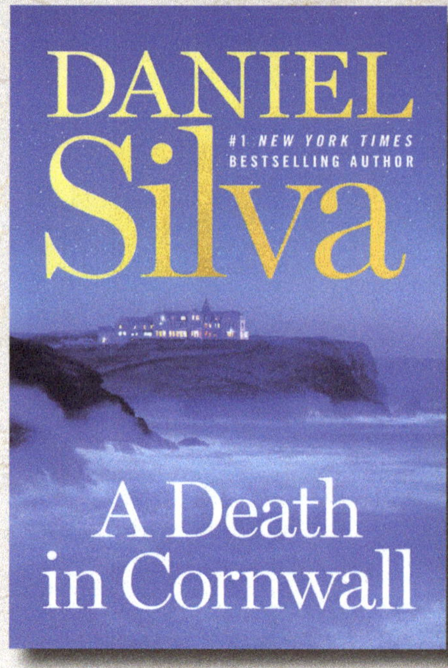

GREAT CIRCLE

by Maggie Shipstead

"Great Circle" is a masterful, inspiring tale of adventure and identity, beautifully written with unforgettable characters and vivid storytelling.

Maggie Shipstead's *Great Circle* is a breathtaking literary achievement that intertwines the lives of two women separated by nearly a century but connected by their unyielding spirit and quest for freedom. This novel showcases Shipstead's prowess as a storyteller, weaving historical and contemporary narratives that captivate and inspire.

The story follows Marian Graves, an intrepid aviator whose life is marked by daring adventures and a relentless pursuit of the skies. From her early days flying in Alaska to her mysterious disappearance while attempting a great circle flight around the globe, Marian's journey is one of courage and resilience. Shipstead's meticulous research and vivid descriptions bring Marian's world to life, making her a character who feels both larger-than-life and deeply human.

Parallel to Marian's story is that of Hadley Baxter, a modern-day actress cast to play Marian in a biopic. Hadley's struggles with fame, identity, and personal demons provide a compelling counterpoint to Marian's narrative. As Hadley delves deeper into Marian's life, she embarks on her own journey of self-discovery. Shipstead skillfully navigates these dual timelines, creating a seamless and engaging narrative.

One of the novel's greatest strengths is its exploration of themes such as freedom, identity, and societal constraints. Marian's defiance of gender norms and her determination to carve out her own path in a male-dominated field are both inspiring and thought-provoking. Similarly, Hadley's struggle to reconcile her public persona with her true self resonates deeply.

Shipstead's prose is both lyrical and precise, capturing the grandeur of the skies and the intimate moments of her characters' lives. "Great Circle" is a profound exploration of living authentically and pursuing one's passions against all odds. This novel will linger in your thoughts long after you've turned the final page.

ALL THE BROKEN PLACES

by John Boyne

A poignant, beautifully written exploration of guilt, redemption, and history's shadows. Boyne's storytelling is both compelling and deeply moving.

John Boyne's *All the Broken Places* is a masterful exploration of guilt, redemption, and the long shadows cast by history. This poignant novel follows the life of Gretel Fernsby, a 91-year-old woman living in London, who harbors a dark secret from her past. As the story unfolds, Boyne skillfully weaves together past and present, revealing the haunting memories of Gretel's childhood in Nazi Germany and her struggle to reconcile with her family's legacy.

Boyne's narrative is both compelling and heart-wrenching, drawing readers into Gretel's internal conflict and the moral complexities she faces. The character development is exceptional, with Gretel portrayed as a deeply flawed yet sympathetic figure. Her interactions with her neighbors and the arrival of a new family in her building serve as catalysts for her to confront her past, leading to moments of profound introspection and emotional revelation.

The novel's pacing is well-balanced, with Boyne maintaining a delicate tension throughout. His prose is elegant and evocative, capturing the nuances of human emotion and the weight of historical trauma. The themes of forgiveness and the possibility of redemption are explored with sensitivity and depth, making *"All the Broken Places"* a thought-provoking read.

One of the novel's strengths is its ability to humanize its characters, presenting them in shades of gray rather than black and white. This nuanced portrayal encourages readers to reflect on the complexities of morality and the impact of history on individual lives.

All the Broken Places is a beautifully written and emotionally resonant novel that will stay with readers long after they turn the final page. John Boyne has crafted a powerful story that speaks to the enduring human capacity for change and forgiveness.

A DEATH IN CORNWALL

by Daniel Silva

A masterful thriller, "A Death in Cornwall" captivat with its intricate plot, vivid settings, and compellin characters. An absolute must-rea

Daniel Silva's latest novel, *A Death in Cornwall*, is a masterful blend of suspense, intrigue, and rich character development that will captivate both long-time fans and new readers alike. Set against the picturesqu yet brooding backdrop of Cornwall, Silva weaves a ta that is as atmospheric as it is thrilling.

The story follows Gabriel Allon, the legendary art restorer and spy, who is drawn into a complex web of deceit and murder. When a prominent art dealer is found dead under mysterious circumstances, Allon is reluctantly pulled from his quiet life in Venice to unravel the truth. What begins as a seemingly straightforward investigation quickly spirals into a labyrinth of secrets involving stolen masterpieces, international conspiracies, and a shadowy adversary from Allon's past.

Silva's writing is as sharp and evocative as ever. Hi meticulous attention to detail brings the Cornish landscape to life, making it almost a character in its own right. The plot is tightly woven, with twists and turns that keep the reader guessing until the very end. Silva' ability to blend historical facts with fiction adds a laye of depth and authenticity to the narrative, making the stakes feel incredibly real.

The character of Gabriel Allon continues to evolve, showing new facets of his personality and skills. His interactions with a cast of well-drawn supporting characters, including his wife Chiara and a host of nev and familiar faces, add emotional weight and complexity to the story.

A Death in Cornwall is a testament to Daniel Silva' prowess as a storyteller. It's a gripping, intelligent thriller that not only entertains but also provokes though about the art world and the murky waters of international espionage. Whether you're a die-hard Silva fan or newcomer to his work, this novel is a must-read.

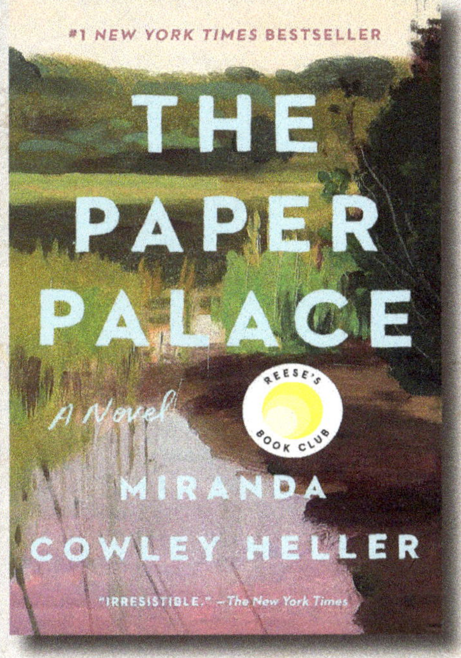

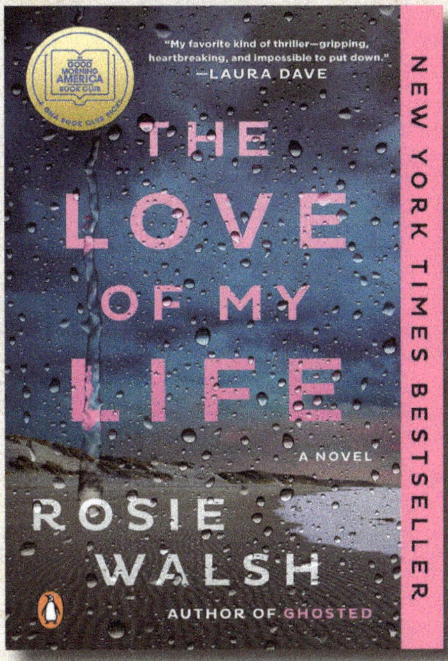

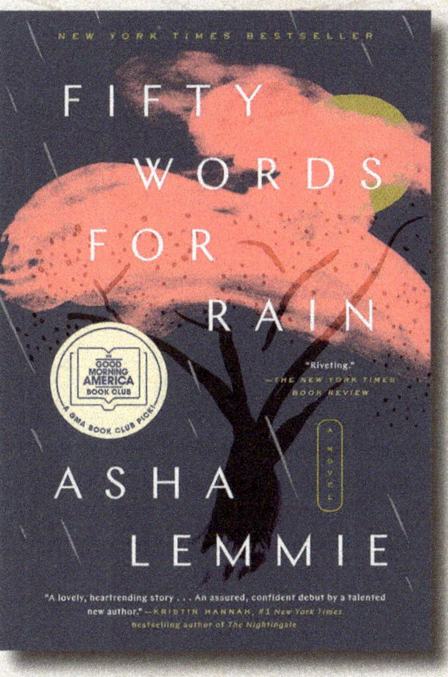

THE PAPER PALACE

by Miranda Cowley Heller

"A thrilling urban fantasy, 'The Reign of the Occult' captivates with its vivid world, dynamic characters, and relentless action."

Miranda Cowley Heller's debut novel, *The Paper Palace*, is a masterful exploration of love, betrayal, and the complexities of human relationships. Set against the backdrop of a rustic summer retreat in Cape Cod, the story unfolds over a single day, interwoven with flashbacks that span fifty years of the protagonist's life.

The narrative centers on Elle Bishop, who finds herself at a crossroads after a passionate encounter with her childhood friend, Jonas. This moment of infidelity forces Elle to confront her past and the choices that have led her to this pivotal point. Heller's writing is both lyrical and evocative, painting vivid pictures of the natural beauty of the Cape and the emotional landscapes of her characters.

One of the novel's greatest strengths is its rich character development. Elle is a deeply flawed yet relatable protagonist, and her internal struggle is portrayed with raw honesty. The supporting characters, from Elle's charming yet distant husband, Peter, to her enigmatic mother, Wallace, are equally well-drawn, adding depth and complexity to the story.

Heller's use of dual timelines is particularly effective, gradually revealing the secrets and traumas that have shaped Elle's life. This structure keeps the reader engaged, as each revelation adds a new layer of understanding to the present-day narrative. The themes of love, loss, and forgiveness are explored with nuance, making the novel both thought-provoking and emotionally resonant.

However, some readers may find the pacing slow at times, and the frequent shifts between past and present can be disorienting. Despite this, *The Paper Palace* is a compelling read that will linger in your mind long after you've turned the last page. Heller's debut is a testament to her storytelling prowess and a promising start to her literary career.

THE LOVE OF MY LIFE

by Rosie Walsh

A beautifully written, emotionally gripping novel that masterfully blends romance and mystery. Rosie Walsh's storytelling is simply unforgettable.

Rosie Walsh's *"The Love of My Life"* is a masterful blend of romance, mystery, and emotional depth that keeps readers hooked from the first page to the last. The novel centers around Emma and Leo, a seemingly perfect couple whose lives are upended when Leo, an obituary writer, discovers startling secrets about Emma's past while researching her life for a piece he hopes never to write.

Walsh's storytelling prowess shines through her intricate plot and well-developed characters. Emma is a compelling protagonist, whose hidden layers are peeled back with each chapter, revealing a complex and relatable woman. Leo's journey from a loving husband to a man grappling with betrayal and confusion is equally gripping. Their relationship, filled with genuine love and palpable tension, forms the heart of the novel.

The narrative is beautifully paced, with Walsh skillfully balancing moments of suspense with poignant reflections on love, trust, and forgiveness. The dual perspectives of Emma and Leo provide a rich, multifaceted view of their relationship and the secrets that threaten to unravel it. Walsh's prose is both lyrical and accessible, making the emotional weight of the story resonate deeply with readers.

One of the standout aspects of *The Love of My Life* is its exploration of identity and the lengths to which people go to protect their loved ones. The twists and turns are expertly crafted, keeping readers guessing until the very end. Walsh's ability to weave a tale that is both heart-wrenching and hopeful is truly commendable.

In summary, *The Love of My Life* is a captivating and emotionally charged novel that showcases Rosie Walsh's talent for creating unforgettable stories. It's a must-read for fans of contemporary fiction and anyone who appreciates a well-told tale of love and redemption.

FIFTY WORDS FOR RAIN

by Asha Lemmie

Fifty Words for Rain is a beautifully written, emotionally gripping tale of resilience, identity, and hope. A truly unforgettable read.

Asha Lemmie's debut novel, "Fifty Words for Rain," is a poignant and beautifully crafted tale that transports readers to post-World War II Japan. The story follows Nori, a biracial child born out of wedlock to a Japanese aristocrat and her African American lover. Abandoned by her mother and left in the care of her strict grandmother, Nori's life is one of confinement and secrecy, reflecting the societal prejudices of the time.

Lemmie's prose is both lyrical and evocative, painting a vivid picture of Nori's internal and external struggles. The author masterfully captures the essence of Nori's resilience and determination as she navigates a world that constantly seeks to diminish her. The character development is exceptional, with Nori's journey from a submissive child to a young woman who dares to dream and defy societal norms being particularly compelling.

The novel's exploration of themes such as identity, family, and the quest for acceptance is both heart-wrenching and inspiring. Lemmie does not shy away from depicting the harsh realities of Nori's life, yet she also infuses the narrative with moments of hope and beauty. The relationship between Nori and her half-brother Akira is especially touching, providing a beacon of light in her otherwise dark world.

Fifty Words for Rain is not just a story about survival; it is a testament to the human spirit's capacity for growth and transformation. Lemmie's ability to weave historical context with a deeply personal story makes this novel a standout. It is a powerful reminder of the importance of perseverance and the enduring quest for self-acceptance.

Asha Lemmie's *Fifty Words for Rain* is a must-read for anyone who appreciates a well-told story of resilience and hope. It is a remarkable debut that promises a bright future for this talented author.

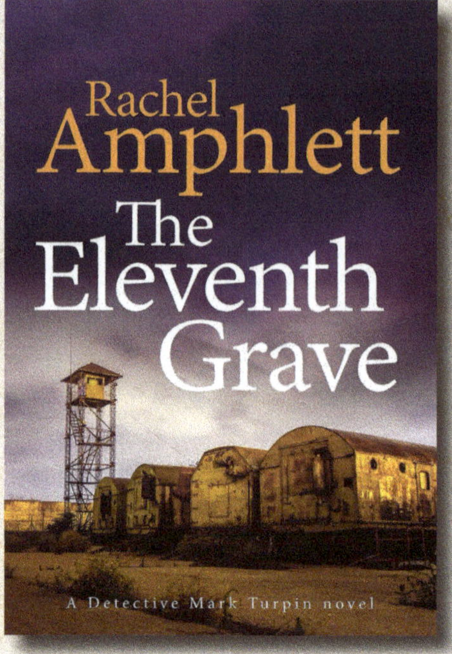

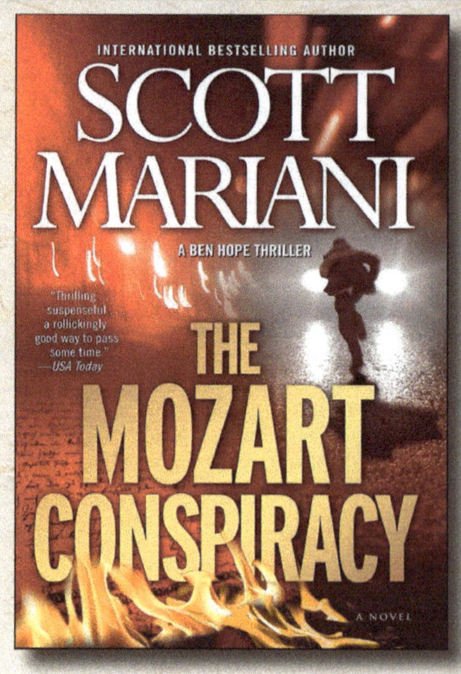

MERELY MORTAL

by Michelle M. Pillow

Merely Mortalenchants with its rich world-building, compelling characters, and a beautifully crafted romance. A magical and heartwarming read!

Michelle M. Pillow's *Merely Mortal*is a delightful foray into a world where fantasy and romance intertwine seamlessly. From the very first page, Pillow's masterful storytelling draws readers into a realm filled with magic, intrigue, and heartwarming relationships.

The protagonist, Elara, is a refreshingly relatable character. Her journey from an ordinary life to discovering her extraordinary heritage is both compelling and inspiring. Pillow does an excellent job of developing Elara's character, making her growth feel natural and earned. The supporting characters, particularly the enigmatic and charming Aiden, add depth and richness to the narrative, creating a dynamic ensemble that keeps the reader engaged.

One of the standout aspects of *Merely Mortal*is Pillow's world-building. The magical elements are intricately woven into the fabric of the story, creating a setting that is both fantastical and believable. The author's vivid descriptions and attention to detail make it easy to visualize the enchanting landscapes and mystical creatures that populate this world.

The romance between Elara and Aiden is beautifully crafted, striking a perfect balance between passion and tenderness. Their relationship evolves organically, with moments of tension and vulnerability that add layers to their connection. Pillow's ability to convey deep emotions through her characters is truly commendable.

However, the pacing of the story occasionally feels uneven. Some sections are richly detailed and immersive, while others rush through key plot points, leaving the reader wanting more. Despite this minor flaw, the overall narrative remains engaging and satisfying.

*Merely Mortal*is a captivating read that will appeal to fans of both fantasy and romance. Michelle M. Pillow has created a magical world that readers will be eager to revisit. With its well-drawn characters and enchanting storyline, this book is a testament to Pillow's talent as a storyteller. Highly recommended for those looking for an escape into a world of magic and love.

THE ELEVENTH GRAVE

by Rachel Amphlett

A poignant, beautifully written exploration of guilt, redemption, and history's shadows. Boyne's storytelling is both compelling and deeply moving.

Rachel Amphlett's *The Eleventh Grave*is a masterful addition to the Detective Kay Hunter series, delivering a gripping narrative that keeps readers on the edge of their seats from start to finish. Amphlett's skillful storytelling and intricate plotting shine through in this latest installment, making it a must-read for fans of crime thrillers.

The story kicks off with a chilling discovery: a body buried in a shallow grave, with clues that suggest a connection to a series of unsolved murders. Detective Kay Hunter and her team are thrust into a complex investigation that tests their limits and uncovers dark secrets lurking beneath the surface. Amphlett's portrayal of Hunter is both compelling and relatable, as she balances the pressures of her professional life with personal challenges.

One of the standout features of *The Eleventh Grave*is Amphlett's ability to create a palpable sense of tension and urgency. The pacing is impeccable, with each chapter ending on a note that compels you to keep reading. The plot twists are well-executed and keep you guessing until the very end, making it difficult to put the book down.

Amphlett's attention to detail and thorough research are evident in the authenticity of the investigative procedures and the depth of the characters. The supporting cast, including Hunter's colleagues and suspects, are well-developed and add richness to the narrative. The dialogue is sharp and realistic, further immersing readers in the story.

*The Eleventh Grave*is a stellar addition to the Detective Kay Hunter series. Rachel Amphlett has once again proven her prowess in crafting a suspenseful and engaging thriller. Whether you're a long-time fan of the series or new to Kay Hunter's world, this book is sure to satisfy your craving for a well-written, edge-of-your-seat mystery. Highly recommended.

THE MOZART CONSPIRACY

by Scott Mariani

A masterful blend of history and suspense, "The Mozart Conspiracy" is an unputdownable thriller that captivates from start to finish.

Scott Mariani's "The Mozart Conspiracy" is an exhilarating blend of historical intrigue and modern-day suspense that will captivate readers from the first page to the last. The novel centers around Ben Hope, an ex-SAS operative turned scholar, who is drawn into a centuries-old mystery involving the death of the legendary composer Wolfgang Amadeus Mozart.

Mariani's storytelling prowess shines through in this meticulously researched and vividly described narrative. The historical backdrop of 18th-century Europe is brought to life with rich detail, immersing readers in a world of secret societies, hidden codes, and long-buried secrets. The author skillfully intertwines historical facts with fiction, creating a tapestry of suspense that is both educational and thrilling.

The character of Ben Hope is particularly compelling. Mariani has crafted a protagonist who is not only skilled and resourceful but also deeply human, with personal struggles and vulnerabilities that add depth to his character. Hope's journey is fraught with danger and deception, and his relentless pursuit of the truth makes for a gripping read.

The plot is intricately woven, with numerous twists and turns that keep readers guessing. Just when you think you have it all figured out, Mariani throws in another curveball, maintaining a high level of suspense throughout. The pacing is perfect, with a balance of action-packed sequences and moments of introspection that allow for character development.

"The Mozart Conspiracy" is more than just a thriller; it's a thought-provoking exploration of history, music, and the lengths to which people will go to uncover—or conceal—the truth. Mariani's ability to blend these elements seamlessly is a testament to his skill as a writer.

"The Mozart Conspiracy" is a must-read for fans of historical thrillers and anyone who enjoys a well-crafted mystery. Scott Mariani has delivered a novel that is not only a page-turner but also a richly rewarding reading experience. This book will leave you breathless and eager for more.

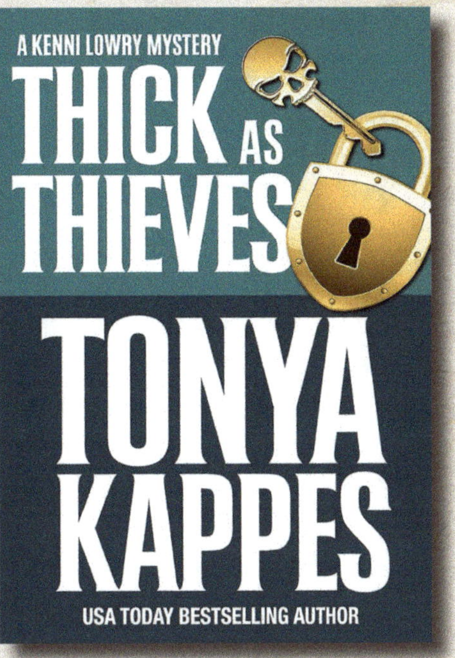

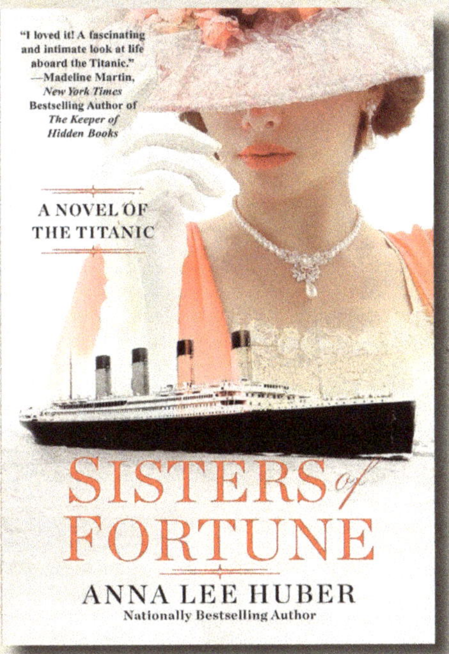

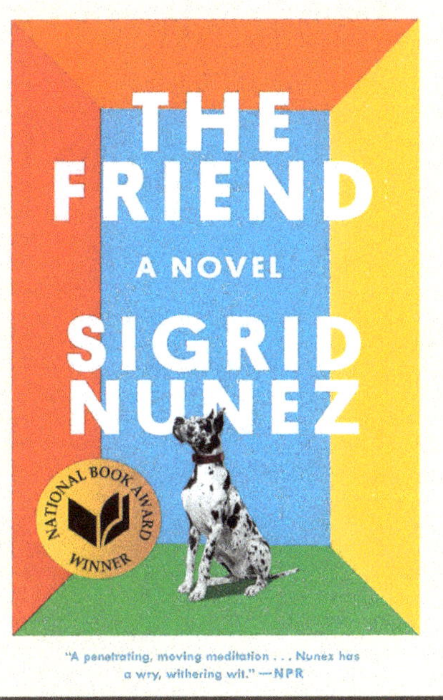

THICK AS THIEVES

by Tonya Kappes

Thick As Thieves is a delightful, suspenseful cozy mystery with charming characters and a captivating Southern setting. Highly recommended!

Thick As Thieves, the latest installment in Tonya Kappes' Kenni Lowry Mystery series, is a delightful blend of Southern charm, humor, and suspense. Set in the quaint town of Cottonwood, Kentucky, this cozy mystery follows Sheriff Kenni Lowry as she navigates a web of secrets, lies, and small-town politics to solve a perplexing murder.

Kappes excels in creating a vivid, engaging setting that feels like a character in its own right. Cottonwood is brought to life with its quirky residents, local gossip, and the ever-present Southern hospitality. The author's attention to detail and her ability to capture the essence of small-town life make the reader feel as though they are part of the community.

Sheriff Kenni Lowry is a compelling protagonist. Her determination, wit, and relatability make her a character readers can root for. The dynamic between Kenni and her ghostly grandfather, Poppa, adds a unique twist to the narrative. Poppa's spectral presence provides both comic relief and valuable insights, making their interactions a highlight of the book.

The plot of *Thick As Thieves*is well-crafted, with enough twists and turns to keep readers guessing until the very end. Kappes skillfully balances the mystery with moments of humor and heart, ensuring that the story remains engaging throughout. The pacing is brisk, and the dialogue is sharp, reflecting the author's knack for capturing the nuances of Southern speech.

One of the strengths of this book is its ensemble cast. The supporting characters are well-developed and add depth to the story. From Kenni's loyal deputy, Finn, to the eccentric townsfolk, each character plays a crucial role in unraveling the mystery.

*Thick As Thieves*is a thoroughly enjoyable read that will appeal to fans of cozy mysteries and Southern fiction. Tonya Kappes has once again delivered a charming, suspenseful, and heartwarming story that leaves readers eagerly anticipating the next adventure in the Kenni Lowry series.

SISTERS OF FORTUNE

by Anna Lee Huber

Sisters of Fortune is a beautifully crafted historical novel, rich in detail and emotion, with unforgettable characters and gripping plot twists.

Anna Lee Huber's *Sisters of Fortune* is a captivating historical novel that masterfully intertwines mystery, romance, and the complexities of familial bonds. Set against the rich backdrop of 19th-century Europe, the story follows the lives of three sisters—Eleanor, Charlotte, and Georgiana—as they navigate the treacherous waters of society, love, and fortune.

Huber's meticulous attention to historical detail is evident from the very first page, immersing readers in the opulent yet perilous world of the Victorian era. The author's ability to weave historical facts with fiction creates a vivid and believable setting that enhances the narrative's authenticity. The sisters' distinct personalities and their evolving relationships are portrayed with depth and nuance, making them relatable and compelling.

Eleanor, the eldest, is a strong and determined character whose sense of duty often conflicts with her personal desires. Charlotte, the middle sister, is a free spirit whose artistic inclinations and romantic entanglements add layers of intrigue to the plot. Georgiana, the youngest, brings a sense of innocence and curiosity that balances the trio. Their individual journeys are skillfully interwoven, creating a tapestry of suspense and emotional resonance.

The novel's pacing is well-executed, with each chapter revealing new twists and turns that keep readers engaged. Huber's prose is elegant and evocative, capturing the essence of the period while maintaining a modern readability. The themes of sisterhood, loyalty, and the pursuit of happiness are explored with sensitivity and insight, making the story both thought-provoking and heartwarming.

Sisters of Fortune is a testament to Anna Lee Huber's talent as a storyteller. It is a must-read for fans of historical fiction and anyone who appreciates a well-crafted tale of love, mystery, and the enduring bonds of family. This novel is sure to leave a lasting impression and is highly recommended for your next literary adventure.

THE FRIEND

by Sigrid Nunez

A beautifully written, deeply moving exploration of grief, friendship, and healing through an unexpected bond with a Great Dane.

Sigrid Nunez's *The Friend* is a poignant and deeply moving exploration of grief, friendship, and the unexpected ways in which life can offer solace. The novel centers around an unnamed narrator who, after the sudden death of her close friend and mentor, finds herself the reluctant caretaker of his Great Dane, Apollo. As she navigates her profound sense of loss, the bond she forms with the dog becomes a source of unexpected comfort and understanding.

Nunez's prose is both elegant and unflinchingly honest, capturing the complexities of human emotion with a rare sensitivity. The narrative seamlessly weaves together reflections on literature, the nature of writing, and the intricacies of human relationships, creating a rich tapestry that resonates on multiple levels. The relationship between the narrator and Apollo is depicted with such tenderness and authenticity that it transcends the typical pet-owner dynamic, becoming a profound meditation on companionship and healing.

The novel delves into the narrator's internal struggles, her memories of her friend, and her reflections on the literary world, all while she grapples with the challenges of caring for a dog that is as large as he is gentle. Apollo, with his silent yet powerful presence, becomes a mirror to the narrator's own journey through grief, offering her a sense of purpose and a new perspective on life.

The Friend is not just a story about loss; it is also a celebration of the enduring power of love and the ways in which it can manifest in our lives. Nunez's ability to convey the depth of her characters' inner worlds makes this novel a deeply affecting read that lingers long after the final page. The book is a testament to the healing power of companionship, whether it comes from a human or an animal, and it beautifully illustrates how connections can help us navigate the darkest times.

Ann Charles Brings Humor, Mystery And Paranormal Mayhem To Life With Her Bestselling Books

By Novelist Post Staff

Photo:USA Today Bestselling Author Ann Charles, crafting thrilling tales packed with adventure, humor, romance, and supernatural surprises.

Exploring The Wit, Wisdom, And Supernatural Secrets Of Ann Charles

Ann Charles discusses blending humor, suspense, and paranormal elements in her bestselling mysteries, shares insights on biology-inspired stories, and encourages aspiring writers to chase their storytelling dreams without fear.

Ann Charles, a storytelling powerhouse, is everything a reader could hope for in an author. With her unique blend of humor, suspense, romance, and just the right dose of supernatural chaos, Ann has carved out her niche in the world of fiction, captivating audiences across the globe. Her books are not merely stories; they are immersive experiences filled with quirky characters, unforgettable adventures, and small-town charm that feels anything but small. As a USA Today Bestselling Author, she's not only mastered the art of entertaining but also the craft of leaving her audience eagerly awaiting the next twist, laugh, or chilling moment.

One of the hallmarks of Ann's writing is her ability to make the intricate interplay of life, death, and survival come alive—whether through ghostly encounters or villainous schemes—drawing readers into worlds that are both enchanting and eerie. Her Deadwood Mystery series, set in the famously haunted town of Deadwood, South Dakota, is a testament to her skill at weaving local history and legends into compelling narratives. But Ann doesn't stop at the supernatural; her stories often explore deeper themes, even biological mysteries, where science seems to tiptoe into the realm of the bizarre.

Ann Charles isn't just an author—she's a storyteller unafraid to delve into the humorous, the dark, and the downright extraordinary. In this exclusive interview, we explore the mind behind the page-turning plots, quirky characters, and paranormal puzzles that have won the hearts of readers everywhere. From biology-inspired thrills to crafting moments of levity amidst suspense, Ann masterfully shows us how science, mystery, and humanity collide. Prepare to be inspired, entertained, and delighted as Ann offers a behind-the-scenes look into the world of her storytelling.

Many of your books feature supernatural or mysterious elements—if you could weave a real biological phenomenon (like bioluminescence, genetic mutations, or animal behavior) into one of your Deadwood mysteries, which would you pick and why?

Bioluminescence is amazing. I was fortunate to witness it myself at the ocean once and will never forget splashing around in the neon blue waves. However, being that the supernatural mysteries I enjoy writing tend to have a sinister edge, I would lean toward genetic mutations caused by a malevolent lifeform from another realm that enters our natural world through a mystical gate or wormhole between worlds.

Biology and mystery both deal with solving puzzles—how do you think the process of unraveling a scientific mystery compares to solving a fictional crime in your books?

A mystery is a mystery, and as with any puzzle, you start with the evidence available. After that, it's one patient step at a time: 1. Gather information. 2. Lay it all out before you. 3. Analyze it. 4. Step away to clear your head so you can return and see patterns. 5. Solve the mystery. That being said, not all mysteries are easily solved. Sometimes the answers lead to further mysteries to solve, giving both the scientist and writer a greater purpose.

Some biological processes can seem stranger than the supernatural (like parasites taking over hosts). Have you ever been inspired by bizarre aspects of biology to create eerie or funny moments in your stories?

It's interesting that you mention parasites and hosts, because that is exactly what happened in one of the books in my Deadwood Mystery series, Never Say Sever in Deadwood. The parasite was delivered via a creature that would crawl through the host's ear canal to reach the brain, where it would begin its new life and slowly take over the host, causing drastic mutations on both mental and physical levels.

Ann Charles is a gifted storyteller whose signature blend of humor, suspense, and paranormal adventures captivates readers everywhere.

If Violet Parker were faced with a villain who used knowledge of biology to commit a crime, what kind of biological twist would you imagine? (Poison, viruses, rare plants, animal behavior, etc.)

Definitely animal behavior. That offers a lot of opportunities to a writer's imagination.

Your books are full of humor alongside suspense. Do you think humor can help readers better digest complex subjects, even in science, much like it eases the darker elements in your mysteries?

I see it this way. When a storyteller uses suspense or darkness to tell a tale, those elements are better contrasted when humor or a smidgen of lightness are interjected periodically. Those elements punctuate the prose, so to speak. If the story doesn't give the reader a break now and then, they'll be exhausted by the end of it all.

Biology often deals with themes of life, death, and survival—core elements in your stories. How consciously do you tie these natural cycles into your plots?

The key to good storytelling is creating a strong plot frame underlying the written scenes and sequels, and then seamlessly weaving the theme and premise (such as those you mentioned and/or others) throughout the narrative and dialogue on the pages. All of this is done in a way that the readers cannot see the story's structure, but they sense it as the tale takes them on an adventure through the pages.

If you had to team up one of your quirky characters with a real scientist or biologist, who would it be and what kind of case would they work on?

I actually have "real" scientists in my stories—I have a geomorphologist in my Jackrabbit Junction series and multiple archaeologists in my Dig Site series. These characters solve mysteries using their scientific knowledge. I love researching for these books because reading through scientific articles is usually fun and always educational.

The town of Deadwood and its environment play a strong role in your books. Have you ever drawn inspiration from local plants, animals, or landscapes in a biological sense to heighten the mystery or atmosphere?

I actually use the real-life town of Deadwood for the setting in my Deadwood Mystery series, so the place itself is part of the inspiration for the stories, including not only its past, but also the many ghosts that live there and their corresponding stories.

Aside from the supernatural, biology has its own "mysteries" that remain unsolved. Is there a biological mystery you personally find fascinating that you'd love to explore in fiction?

I am waiting to hear or read that something biologically intriguing has emerged from the melting ice near the Earth's poles. I think that the change in climate will offer many opportunities for those fiction writers who enjoy writing mysteries, thrillers, and horror.

Stepping away from biology—what has been the most rewarding (and most challenging) part of your journey as a bestselling author, and what advice would you give aspiring authors who want to blend their passions (whether for science, humor, or mystery) into their writing?

It's definitely meeting all of the interesting and kind readers and writers along the way on my continued journey to provide fun stories full of mystery, adventure, and joy (along with a few cringes). When I think back through the highlights so far, it always comes back to the people who I've met and experienced shared moments of laughter and smiles. The most challenging is keeping up on the marketing front in this everchanging world of technology and AI.

As for advice for aspiring authors—it's just this: Don't give up. People need stories. They feed our souls and give life more meaning.

Ann Charles delivers yet another thrilling, laugh-out-loud ride with *Cops and Clobbers in Deadwood.* Packed with quirky twists, paranormal thrills, and Violet Parker's mischievous antics, this book is a delightful chaos of cops, clocks, and comedy. The suspense keeps you hooked, while the humor lightens every dark corner. Book 14 proves why the Deadwood series remains a fan favorite.

Bioluminescence is amazing... but I would lean toward genetic mutations caused by a malevolent lifeform from another realm."

Ann Charles

John Reinhardt Finds Humor And Wisdom In Everyday Life Through His Captivating Books

By Novelist Post Staff

Photo: *John Reinhardt enjoys a serene moment with his wife, Lynn, showcasing their shared journey and enduring togetherness.*

John Reinhardt is a literary craftsman whose journey defies conventional boundaries, transitioning from an illustrious career in book design to becoming an author who captures life's everyday truths with wit and wisdom. For more than fifty years, John shaped the printed pages of countless authors, honing a meticulous eye for detail and a creative flair that enriched the works of others. Today, his own voice shines brightly in the literary world—both sharp and profoundly relatable—delivering stories that blend humor, reflection, and a genuine understanding of humanity's quirks and complexities.

Reinhardt's books, affectionately dubbed "My Crazy Books," invite readers to look differently at life's ordinary moments—whether it's navigating the frustrations of driving, the chaos of shopping, or the nuances of golf. With his characteristic humor and sharp observations, John reminds us not only to laugh at life's absurdities but also to reflect on how our behavior impacts others. His ability to elevate the minutiae of everyday life into compelling narratives speaks to his deep understanding of human behavior and his desire to help us all be a little better, a little kinder.

Exploring Human Behavior With Humor And Insight

John Reinhardt shares his journey from book designer to author, blending humor and reflection to tackle everyday annoyances like driving, shopping, and etiquette in his insightful "Crazy" book series.

From his days in an Army uniform to his love for marathons, rowing, and guitar-playing, John's rich, multifaceted life infuses every chapter of his writing. Whether wryly critiquing bad driving habits or exploring overlooked social etiquette, his work carries an unmistakable authenticity born from his own experiences and adventures. As John continues to add to his "Crazy" series and share his reflections on his extraordinary career in design, his passion for creativity and storytelling remains undiminished—an inspiration not only to writers but to anyone seeking to turn life's moments, big or small, into lasting contributions. This interview shines a spotlight on the mind behind the stories, offering readers a glimpse into the heart and humor of John Reinhardt's work.

What inspired you to shift from designing books to writing your own?

After nearly fifty years of designing thousands of books for others, it was inevitable that I would eventually write one (or more) of my own. I have always been fascinated with human behavior in public settings and with my love for driving, it became obvious I needed to write a book about bad driving situations. I enjoyed writing this book so much, I knew it was just the beginning.

How did your experiences as a book designer influence the way you approached writing and structuring your own books?

I have worked with so many authors and editors over

the years, and I have learned from them. My approach is like designing a book. I write down thoughts as I think of them. Much like creating a quilt, I write small pieces and eventually those pieces will begin to connect to one another. When all my "pieces" are properly connected I begin to "sew" the book together from start to finish, filling in the gaps as I go.

What motivated you to focus on everyday annoyances like driving and shopping for your first books?

Driving is a dangerous activity and if done wrong, the result can be deadly. I take driving seriously and when I'm behind the wheel, I focus all my attention on everything going on around me. I apply this attitude when I am in public and around others. Whether it be walking through an aisle in a grocery store, playing golf, on an airplane, or just being with others, I pay attention to the situation and anticipate actions and reactions. I see a lot of things we all can do better to help others enjoy the same experiences. And as a result, I want to share my observations, and suggestions with others in hopes these books can help their lives be better.

> John Reinhardt brilliantly transforms life's ordinary frustrations into engaging stories, inspiring readers with humor, wisdom, and thought-provoking insights on human behavior.

How do you balance humor with serious safety or etiquette messages in your writing?

Most people know me for telling jokes. There are times, when telling a story, people don't know whether it is serious, or whether it's going to be a joke. This prompts them to be curious. I think people are more willing to listen to something when there is humor involved. I love to laugh and smile, so I begin each of the topics in my books with a humorous, light-hearted comment to help get the reader interested in what may be a serious subject to follow.

Were there any particular events or observations that directly led to stories in your books?

Nothing in particular, but rather the frequency with which these behaviors and situations occurred. I am easily frustrated and disappointed in how so many people inconsiderately conduct themselves in public. Many people move about as if they have blinders on, not paying attention to those around them. There are so many simple things we can do to help make others' lives better.

What was it like collaborating with an editor and illustrator for your first authorial project?

Like anything else, working with someone who knows me makes an enormous difference. I have been working with an amazing editor, Kathleen Strattan, for more than thirty years. We've become close friends during that time. She knows what it is I am trying to say and the "voice" in which I am saying it. Therefore, instead of just getting standard editorial guidance, she makes suggestions/edits based on my personality. My books are not just perceptions, but "my" perceptions. This is important to me.

The illustrator for my cover images, Malane Newman, is also amazing. I write a list of things I'd like to see in the illustration, and it is like she is reading my mind. She nails it!

Did your military background shape your approach to identifying and organizing the behaviors you critique?

I am sure my time in the Army has helped me to be critical in the things I, and others, do. One thing that has stuck with me since basic training was to always criticize yourself first before criticizing others. Make sure you are doing things properly before calling out someone else.

How do your hobbies, like go-karting and guitar playing, influence your creativity or writing process?

Most of the things I enjoy doing have some creative element to them. There are standard ways of doing things, but I am always looking to see if there is a better way, or a unique way that might produce a different and more successful or advantageous result. I have always been interested in everything, and I have designed books on just about every subject possible. I am a curious person, and I enjoy looking beyond the surface of things I see and do.

Do you have plans to expand "My Crazy Books" into other areas of everyday life?

So far, I have published "Crazy" books on driving, shopping, and golf. Flying, Cruising, and Dining will follow in the next few months. I am also working on a book about my life and book design career which will focus on my experiences and lessons I have learned in my journey through life, hoping these stories will help others in similar situations.

What advice would you give to other designers or creatives who are thinking about writing their first book?

I am far from an expert on writing, so I rely heavily on my editor to help me get the books to read properly. This is especially important. Just like a proper book design, you want the book to be read in such a way you don't know you're reading but rather visualizing a movie inside your head. If the design or writing is not right, the reader will find it difficult to be fully immersed in the "story." Find an editor you like and who knows you. Work together to get your book right. And let others read it along the way. Their reactions will be invaluable.

> *After fifty years of designing books, it was inevitable that I would eventually write one—or more—of my own.*
>
> **John Reinhardt**

Ron Lamberson Inspires Readers Through Thrilling Adventures and Intergalactic Escapes

Ron Lamberson shares his journey from HR professional to novelist, discussing how global travel, music, and bold imagination shape his award-winning thrillers, sci-fi adventures, and Kilimanjaro Club mysteries.

PHOTO: Ron Lamberson at home in Colorado, crafting adventures and charting intergalactic punk worlds, one page at a time.

Award-Winning Novelist Shares New Worlds, Memorable Characters, And Creative Inspirations

By Carly Preston

Few writers can so effortlessly transport readers across continents and galaxies like Ron Lamberson. With an impressive catalog spanning award-winning thrillers, gripping adventures, and intergalactic punk odysseys, Lamberson has cemented himself as a titan of immersive storytelling. His Kilimanjaro Club novels blend exotic locales with razor-sharp mysteries, while *Heavy Metal Moon* launches readers into a rock-fueled sci-fi universe filled with bold creativity and electric tension. Whether unraveling the mythology of a clandestine society or taking cues from his global travels to craft stunning settings, Lamberson's vivid imagination and relentless pursuit of authenticity shine on every page.

Beyond the page, Ron Lamberson's journey is just as inspiring. Transitioning from the corporate grind of HR to life as a bestselling novelist, he channels his experiences with corporate machinations, cultural exploration, and musical obsessions into his dynamic narratives. His stories are as layered and textured as his own journey—from globetrotting adventures to head-banging concert nights. In this exclusive interview, we dive into the mind of a writer who dares to blend adrenaline, myth, and music into unforgettable fiction. Get ready to explore the creative brilliance of Ron Lamberson—an author who invites you not just to read, but to explore, dream, and wander alongside his unforgettable characters.

In The Poachers of Immortality, you blend adventure with myth—what inspired the international Immortality poaching plot and how did your travel experiences shape its vivid settings?

The book series is grounded in adventure and international settings. My family has special ties to China, so after writing "A Grave Invitation," I knew I wanted to anchor the next book in China. It's a location many Americans haven't visited but are curious about. I love being able to relive my travel experiences to places like The Great Wall, Beijing, and Guangzhou. Weaving the incredible cultural aspects of China, Italy, or Kenya into my books drives my writing.

A Grave Invitation launches the Kilimanjaro Club series—how did you develop the dynamic between its amateur sleuths amid exotic locales?

When I write, I disappear into the characters. It's like being transported into a movie. Visiting a new or unfamiliar location ramps up the stakes. Not only do the characters have to solve a problem, find something, or rescue someone, they have to do it in a place that's exotic and maybe a little uncomfortable. That's thrilling and dangerous. When I put myself in the character's head, I see what they see, feel what they feel, and respond. It's an adventure for me, too.

The Mythos of Malcolm dives deeper into your Kilimanjaro world—how did you expand mythology and character arcs based on fan feedback from the first two books?

I had a lot of people telling me, "We want

more about the old guys!" Bailey Honeybourne and Parnell Sumner are popular, and I love writing about them. As I established backstories for the Kilimanjaro Club and its members, I knew I would spend time telling some of the earlier stories. I had a great time making that happen in book three.

Heavy Metal Moon offers a sci fi punk vibe—what drew you to explore intergalactic punk, and how did music influence the world building?

The germ for "Heavy Metal Moon" came to me while I was finishing "The Poachers of Immortality." I was driving home from work, listening to Sirius radio, and heard "Negasonic Teenage Warhead" by Monster Magnet for the first time. It was released in 1995, but this was 2018. Aside from just being an awesome banger, I loved the lyrics, and my first thought was, "What would an intergalactic rock band look like?" I wanted to root it in something familiar, so the idea of an Earthling leading this band came next. Writing that book has been my favorite creative endeavor.

Your novels combine meticulous locale detail with action—how does your travel to 30+ countries feed into crafting those immersive settings?

Again, for me, visiting a new country is an adventure. I'm constantly thinking of how my travels can have a place in the stories I write. They are homages to the locations I've explored. It's the voluminous histories that blow me away. I want to create a clear visual for the reader, in the hope that they will feel a tinge of what I experience when I'm there. It's akin to cinematography. A compelling story in a mysterious, beautiful location adds another dimension to the experience.

Ron Lamberson skillfully combines vivid detail, gripping plots, and compelling characters to deliver novels that transport readers to unforgettable worlds.

Having transitioned from HR professional to award winning novelist, how did your corporate background inform the themes or character development in your recent thrillers?

Working in HR is an introduction to corporate villainy. I saw the very worst in people, in all levels of an organization, and often at the top. Narcissism, greed, patriarchy—they're elements that can be the foundation for the most nefarious villains. It's been very cathartic for me to write out some of the trauma I accumulated.

You've produced engaging book trailers—how do you approach visual storytelling differently for A Grave Invitation versus The Poachers of Immortality?

I'm a huge fan of movie trailers. The more mysterious, the better. It goes back to immersing myself in the story. What elements of the individual books appear to me? How can I provide a glimpse to a potential reader? Plus, it's just a blast creating something visual from the writing.

As a lifelong concert goer and Guitar novice, how has your musical passion (Nine Inch Nails, Toto) influenced rhythm or tone in your latest books?

I prefer to listen to music when I write. I listened to Nine Inch Nails exclusively when I wrote "A Grave Invitation," and the texture of the music helped transport me to the action in the book. With the later books, I've mixed it up a bit. I try to find music that matches the tone of what I'm writing at that time. For the 1950s segments of "The Mythos of Malcolm," I listened to jazz and big band. For "Heavy Metal Moon," it was more NIN, a frequent dose of Monster Magnet, plus some prog rock. I'm working on the follow up to "Heavy Metal Moon," and I'm always listening to this awesome compilation created for Oga's Cantina at Disney's Star Wars Galaxy's Edge.

With an MBA and creative writing degree, how do analytical skills and storytelling inform one another in constructing your complex recent narratives?

I mistakenly abandoned my analytical skills when I wrote "A Grave Invitation" and the first draft of "The Poachers of Immortality." I didn't start with an outline. I thought I was a pantser. I got lucky with the first book—the story worked. But I had to rewrite the second book with a detailed outline to get the pacing right. From that point on, I've embraced the outline. I give myself a lot of leeway and always stray from the initial path, but it keeps me on track.

What key piece of advice would you offer aspiring authors based on your journey from HR to bestselling novelist in both adventure and sci fi?

Stop making excuses. Many have said it before, but write every day—250 words. Soon, you'll have to claw yourself away from the keyboard or your pen. And write the stories you are passionate about.

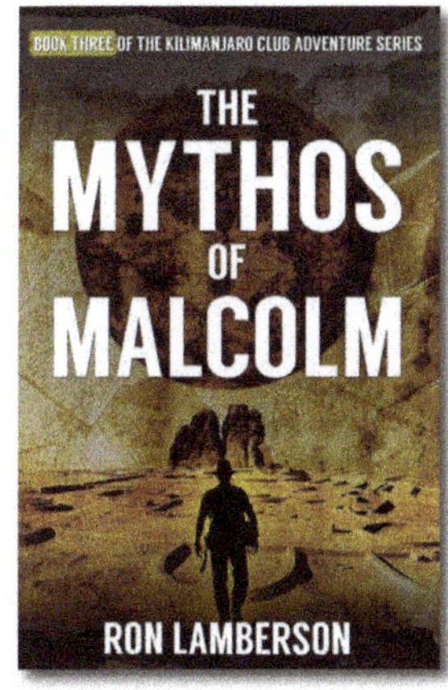

Ron Lamberson's *The Mythos of Malcolm* is a masterful blend of gripping adventure, intricate family dynamics, and vivid historical detail. The dual timelines are seamlessly intertwined, creating a thrilling narrative full of twists and compelling characters. Fans of mystery and exploration will be captivated by this dazzling addition to the Kilimanjaro Club series.

Working in HR is an introduction to corporate villainy—narcissism and greed inspired some of my most nefarious characters.

– Ron Lamberson

Cassidy Carson Inspires Romance Readers With Stories That Blend Adventure, Emotion And Timeless Love

By Novelist Post Staff

Photo: *Cassidy Carson: A Passionate Storyteller Infusing Love, Adventure, And Creativity Into Every Page*

There are certain authors whose works don't just tell a story—they create a world, invite you to step inside, and remind you why you fell in love with reading in the first place. Cassidy Carson is undoubtedly among that special group. With her heartfelt romances and adventurous plots, she bridges the gap between escapism and emotional truth, crafting tales that resonate deeply with readers. Her journey as a writer is nothing short of inspiring, from her humble beginnings penning stories on an electric typewriter gifted by her husband to becoming one-half of a powerhouse creative duo with JT Hume, her lifelong partner and collaborator. Their co-authored novel *From Tundra to Tiara* offers readers a compelling blend of romance and wilderness adventure, while her forthcoming paranormal romance series, *Restless Spirits*, promises intrigue and unexpected introspection, tapping into themes of aging and rediscovery.

Cassidy's unique ability to draw from her rich, multi-faceted life experience—whether it's her love of history, her creative pursuits like painting and acting, or her deep connection to northern Nevada—imbues her characters with authenticity and complexity. Her belief in "love conquering all" radiates through her narratives, reminding us of the beauty in vulnerability and the strength in human connection. Few authors can balance heart-pounding adventure with heartfelt emotion the way Cassidy does, and her dedication to the craft, coupled with her generosity of spirit, shines in every word.

In this interview, Cassidy Carson not only delves into the stories behind her books but also offers insight into her creative process, her partnership with JT, and the life lessons that inspire her themes. Whether you're a long-time fan or a curious newcomer, her words will leave you feeling inspired and eager to turn the page. For those who believe that romance is more than just a genre—it's a celebration of the human spirit—Cassidy Carson is an author you won't want to miss.

Exploring Love, Adventure And Creativity In The Heartfelt Worlds Of Cassidy Carson

Cassidy Carson shares insights into her writing journey, co-authoring with JT Hume, balancing romance and adventure, and crafting heartfelt stories inspired by a rich life of creativity and love.

What inspired you to write "From Tundra to Tiara"?

Throughout our marriage, my husband and I have been fans of action-romance movies like Romancing the Stone and Jewel of the Nile because the comedic light-hearted tones of these films speak to our personalities. As we were leaving the theater after seeing The Lost City we decided to try our hand at writing something similar. The main difference between "From Tundra to Tiara" and the movies we enjoy is that none of our main characters are authors; Lexie is a veterinarian technician in training while Travis is an ex-Navy SEAL turned sled-dog racer.

Can you share your experience of co-writing a book with your husband, JT Hume?

The project turned out to be an eye-opening one. JT and I are in synch with each other in almost everything except writing because I'm a plotter and he's a pantser. In this case, JT and I talked out general story elements without creating a formal structure in advance. I then wrote the first chapter from Lexie's POV, JT responded with chapter two in Travis' POV, and we went back and forth until we finished the draft. The story flowed well and I appreciated not dealing with the normal writers block or messy middle frustration. We enjoyed writing together so much that we have at least a couple more collaborations planned.

> Cassidy Carson's vivid storytelling, authentic characters, and emotional depth remind us why romance is timeless, captivating, and empowering.

How does your background in creative pursuits like painting, acting, and dancing influence your writing?

My hobbies feed my creative spirit. Sketching and painting help me to visualize background or character elements, acting gives me the chance to explore emotions, while music and dancing provide me with a sense of rhythm and flow. I feel these pursuits make me a more well-rounded writer and I hope some of my enjoyment of them feeds my characters.

Why did you choose northern Nevada as your home, and does the location influence your stories?

To be honest, I didn't like Nevada when I first moved here because the surroundings seemed stark compared to my childhood home in the central valley of California. After JT and I married we moved away and lived in Nebraska for seven years and Japan for three. When we returned to Carson City, I came to love the history, individualism, and open vistas of the Silver State. The seasonal moodiness of the vast skies and comforting embrace of the surrounding hills makes a great setting for a wide variety of stories. That's one reason I chose the nearby community of Virginia City as the location for my upcoming paranormal romance.

What challenges did you face while developing the characters of Travis and Lexie in your latest novel?

Balancing real life and fiction turned out be the hardest part of creating Travis and Lexie. Since JT and I each wrote one character, we needed to step back from them because we wanted to be sure the couple had a life of their own. Our experiences and personalities might help shape them but should not match so much that the book became autobiographical!

How do you balance romance and adventure in your stories?

A true romance focuses on the developing relationship between the main characters while I feel adventure should be like cake frosting: a little can go a long way. The dangers faced in the remote Alaskan wilderness happen in the early chapters of "From Tundra to Tiara" because they helped Travis and Lexie to bond in a way they might not in a more conventional environment. Later in the book, the physical adventures fade and the romantic elements take center stage as the couple try to figure out if their relationship can survive in the real world.

What inspired the plot and themes of "#passionrestored, Restless Spirits Book One"?

Reflecting on my past inspired my upcoming paranormal romance. As we age, most of us realize life doesn't always turn out as planned and this how the main characters in "#passionrestored" connect. While Angela Moran and Nicholas Samson come from different backgrounds, both feel they've wasted the best years of their lives. The situations complicating their growing relationship are based the idea that we can't always trust our perceptions of the world. Writing about people navigating the aging process is a way for me to try to understand my own thoughts on the subject and I hope this book will be an entertaining way for readers to do the same.

Can you talk about the creative process behind building the Alaskan wilderness setting in "From Tundra to Tiara"?

We chose the remote location as a way of showing that both Travis and Lexie are hiding from life for different reasons. The harsh beauty of Alaska seemed a good backdrop to the differences between the main characters as Travis is comfortable in his environment whereas Lexie is a little out of her element. Alaska is also a direct contrast to the more cosmopolitan European setting described later in the book.

How has your belief in "love conquering all" shaped the stories you write?

True love is kind and selfless so my characters do their best to find a balance between what they want and what's best for their partner. They need to learn and grow as people in order to face all the challenges they'll face over the course of the story. If they aren't able to find a balance, then something's wrong with the relationship and the reader won't believe in a happily ever after.

What advice would you give to aspiring authors looking to explore the romance genre?

Read a lot of romances to figure out which sub-genres and tropes you prefer because those will be the ones you find the easiest to write. Don't worry too much about following current popular trends if you want your stories to be timeless. Most important of all, be sure to have fun with your stories because that will make them more enjoyable for readers.

Cassidy Carson's *#passionrestored* is a beautifully eerie and emotionally rich paranormal romance set in the atmospheric Virginia City, Nevada. Angela and Nicholas's unlikely connection, intertwined with lingering spirits and tragic pasts, creates a compelling blend of mystery and heartfelt emotion. Carson masterfully balances supernatural intrigue with a touching exploration of love, second chances, and self-discovery. If you enjoy romance with a spooky twist, this enchanting *debut of the* Restless Spirits series is a must-read.

True love is kind and selfless... characters grow to face challenges, creating a believable happily ever after.

Cassidy Carson

Anxious for Love by Gina Conroy is a delightful, slow-burn romance brimming with humor, heart, and sizzling chemistry. Charlee and Maxwell's journey from reluctant allies to something more is captivating and refreshing. With witty banter, relatable conflicts, and a backdrop of Hollywood chaos, this romcom is perfect for fans of feel-good love stories. A charming and satisfying read that leaves you smiling!

An Inspiring Conversation About Writing, Community, And The Power Of Every Voice

Gina Conroy Uncovers the Journey of Storytelling and Mentorship

Gina Conroy shares her transformative journey as a writer, mentor, and author, emphasizing the importance of community and unlocking individual potential.

by Hazel Ivy | LONDON

Gina Conroy embodies the spirit of creativity and resilience, proving that the journey of a writer can be as transformative as the stories they tell. From her early days of penning thoughts in a diary to becoming a published author, Gina has dedicated her life to unlocking the voices of others through mentorship and instruction. Her novels reflect a unique blend of humor, faith, and intricate storytelling that resonates with readers, making her an invaluable asset to the literary community.

In her latest works, *"Digging Up Death"* and the upcoming *"Anxious for Love,"* Gina delves into complex character dynamics and thought-provoking narratives that compel readers to reflect on their own lives. Her ability to weave together suspenseful plots with relatable themes showcases her gift for understanding the human experience. Through her engaging dialogues and richly developed characters, she invites us into a world where every story matters and where the journey toward self-discovery is fraught with both adventure and humor.

Mosaic Digest is proud to feature this insightful interview with Gina Conroy, where she shares her inspirations and the lessons learned along her journey. Her passion for writing and commitment to nurturing aspiring authors highlights the importance of community in the creative process. Whether you are an established writer or just beginning your literary pursuits, Gina's insights will inspire you to embrace your unique voice and confidently share your stories with the world. Gina Conroy embodies the spirit of creativity and resilience, proving that the journey of a writer can be as transformative as the stories they tell. From her early days of penning thoughts in a diary to becoming a published author, Gina has dedicated her life to unlocking the voices of others through mentorship and instruction. Her novels reflect a unique blend of humor, faith, and intricate storytelling that resonates with readers, making her an invaluable asset to the literary community.

Your journey from receiving your first diary in second grade to becoming a published author is inspiring. How did those early experiences shape your passion for storytelling, and what pivotal moments propelled you toward a career in writing?

Growing up, I didn't have a voice. I observed the world around me, keeping my thoughts to myself, unsure if the world would welcome them. At eight years old, my diary became my safe space, allowing me to express myself freely—heart and soul—without judgment. As I grew, encouraging teachers helped build my confidence and inspired my creativity, validating that I indeed have a gift of writing. In high school, I found the courage to share my words publicly through the school newspaper, eventually leading me to study journalism in college.

Although I always loved fiction, I struggled with crafting a novel until post-college inspiration struck while I sat in church listening to a scripture I heard hundreds of times. That's when I began my first book yet to be published.

Joining a critique group opened my eyes to how much I had to learn—and set me on a path of learning. Attending writing conferences and getting to know wonderful writers, editors, and agents was invaluable. Because of their support, I didn't quit when times got tough. Today, I'm a published novelist, writing coach, and tutor because of all my experiences, and I've taken the techniques and principles I learned as an author and created resources to help writers, young and old. My teaching began with a writing course called Release the Novel in You which is now a workbook available on Amazon and grew in 2020 when students were stuck at home during the pandemic. That's when I developed more creative writing courses that I now teach to all ages online and through video format.

You've founded platforms like Writer... Interrupted to mentor busy writers. What motivated you to create these communities, and how have they impacted both your personal growth and the journeys of the writers you've mentored?

Years ago, as a young mother homeschooling four kids while managing a home and pursuing writing, I desperately sought advice from other "successful" writing parents. I was overwhelmed, to say the least. That search led me to create the Writer...Interrupted community, hoping to learn how to balance it all. I started blogging, connecting with other writers, and interviewing busy, successful authors who were "interrupted" to uncover their strategies. Over time, after interviewing hundreds of busy writers, Writer...Interrupted became more than just a blog—it became a community where interrupted writers, like me, could share struggles and insights on how to balance writing with other life responsibilities like homeschooling, caretaking, and health. We blogged insights and tips to encourage ourselves and other writers who were struggling to do it all. Little did I know back when I had a friend write the "caretaking and writing" column that I would be in the thick of it, ten years later.

Through this journey, I've grown as both a writer and mentor, realizing every season of life brings its challenges, but it's the people who are there with you, helping you through that makes the difference. I haven't had one mentor that carried me through the years, like some writers. Instead, I've had different people show up with what I needed at the right time to get me to the next level. That's what I strive to be for new writers.

Balancing multiple roles—author, teacher, writing coach, mother, and caregiver—requires exceptional time management and dedication. What strategies have you developed to maintain this balance, and how do these roles influence and enrich your writing?

The biggest strategy I can offer is to change your perspective about life balance and trying to do it all. As I've matured, I've realized balance isn't about doing it all at the same time—it's about focusing on what matters most in each season of life. After my divorce and then becoming a caregiver to my mom with dementia, I struggled emotionally and financially. Traditional planning methods didn't work for me, especially as I've come to understand my neurodivergent tendencies. But I knew things were out of balance in my life. I could feel it in my body.

I created the Life Balance Workbook to track the areas of my life that mattered most to me—career, family, finances, personal

Gina Conroy's creativity and dedication inspire writers to pursue their dreams and amplify their unique voices in the literary world.

Gina Conroy, a passionate novelist and mentor, sharing her insights on storytelling and the writing journey.
Photo by Nicolas Conroy

"My diary became my safe space, allowing me to express myself freely—heart and soul—without judgment."

Gina Conroy

Sharon Varney Shares the Heart Behind Her Award-Winning Children's Book

by Carine O'Leary

Photo: *Sharon Varney, award-winning author of OH LITTLE ONE, WHO WILL YOU BE?, enjoying a peaceful moment outdoors beneath a leafy tree, reflecting the warmth and imagination in her storytelling..*

Sharon Varney writes with the kind of warmth that only comes from a life steeped in love, reflection, and wonder. Her storytelling is deeply rooted in generational connection—memories of raising children, the joy of becoming a grandparent, and the timeless ritual of reading together. With OH LITTLE ONE, WHO WILL YOU BE?, she offers a heartfelt glimpse into how stories can become anchors, gently guiding little ones as they begin to explore who they are and who they might one day become.

The sincerity in Sharon's words is unmistakable. She doesn't write from a distance—she writes from the heart, shaped by lived experience and a profound appreciation for everyday moments. The gentle humor of a toddler's imagination, the quiet awe of watching a child discover something for the first time—these are the sparks that fuel her creative vision. Her background as an educator only deepens her understanding of what stories can offer to young readers, not just in words, but in confidence and care.

In her debut, she invites readers into a world both specific and universal, where children are reminded they are seen, valued, and unconditionally loved. OH LITTLE ONE, WHO WILL YOU BE? is not only a beautifully illustrated journey through childhood curiosity—it is a reassuring embrace for any child still discovering who they are meant to be.

Sharon Varney Shares the Heart Behind Her Award-Winning Children's Book

Award-winning author Sharon Varney opens up about the inspiration behind her heartfelt debut picture book, the joys of grandparenting, and her hopes for a new generation of young readers.

What inspired you to write OH LITTLE ONE, WHO WILL YOU BE?

The inspiration for Oh Little One, Who Will You Be? came from the most joyful news: becoming grandparents. The overwhelming sense of love and happiness that filled our hearts immediately sparked my desire to capture their story. It's incredibly rewarding to watch my grandchildren growing, exploring, and discovering, and to see my own children embrace their roles as new parents. I'm thrilled that readers of all ages are connecting with the hopeful and empowering message.

How did your own experiences as a parent and grandparent shape the story?

As young parents, we were figuring our way through life, just like many do. We encouraged an excitement for reading, starting with a small library for bedtime stories which grew over the years. When home game consoles became a distraction, we made it a fun ritual to take regular trips to bookstores where our kids picked their own books and occasionally received special perks.

When we became grandparents, a passion for nurturing a brighter future for our grandchildren was heartwarming. It was a wonderful moment to begin sharing my observations as they play and explore, constantly wondering what imaginative worlds they're building in their minds. A fun way to bring our family's reading tradition to life in a new way.

What message do you hope children take away from your book?

The core message I hope all readers take away from Oh Little One, Who Will You Be? is simple: "Be happy being you!" The book aims to show that while we are all wonderfully different, we are also connected by shared experiences—good and bad. I want to encourage every reader to recognize their potential and to know they can make a positive impact in our world. It's also about understanding that there will always be people who see them for who they truly are and accept them unconditionally.

Can you tell us about your collaboration with illustrator Anthony Richichi?

My collaboration with Anthony Richichi was truly amazing! It all began with an impromptu, chance meeting at our local arts and crafts festival. I was telling myself I wasn't ready to discuss my book, which was still a work in progress, but our paths crossed for a reason.

> Sharon Varney writes with heartfelt sincerity, crafting tender, imaginative stories that inspire children while honoring the beauty of family and belonging.

Anthony is a modern-day renaissance man—an artist, illustrator, actor, playwright, and musician. I'm looking forward to working with him again.

I also have to commend Vicki Addesso Dodd and Saratoga Springs Publishing LLC. As my publisher, Vicki's boutique publishing company promoted a welcoming atmosphere. Both Anthony and Vicki were fantastic listeners, demonstrating a genuine understanding that this was a deeply personal story for my grandchildren, with every spread connected to them and our extended family. They offered great suggestions while always respecting my vision.

(Also, special thanks to Aimee D., graphic artist and Toni A-S., editor.)

How did you feel when your book won five major awards?

Winning five major awards for Oh Little One, Who Will You Be? has been a fabulously surprising and ecstatic experience! I am so thrilled by the widespread recognition from esteemed organizations such as The BookFest Awards, the International Impact Book Awards, and the Outstanding Creators Awards.

This book was a labor of love. Every character and every dream explored within its pages holds a real connection.

What was the most challenging part of writing a children's picture book?

For me, the most challenging part of writing Oh Little One, Who Will You Be? was balancing my personal, family-inspired vision with relatability for all young readers. While the initial spark came directly from observing my children and grandchildren, I wanted to create a book inspired by those cherished moments, ensuring my family could hold dear for years to come. The real challenge was taking those special times and crafting them into universal themes.

What age group did you have in mind when creating the story?

When we became grandparents, the idea of writing this children's book was planted like a seed. My goal was to create an engaging and joyful children's story, primarily for ages birth to seven.

The overall theme reflects the wonder we feel as we witness a child's "firsts" and ponder their future possibilities through interactions and play. I truly believe early reading to children is key; even the youngest listeners are captivated by the vibrant illustrations and absorb parts of the story. Soon, little ones begin to "pretend read"—by simply turning pages themselves. These are delightful stages my grandchildren are currently enjoying, making happy sounds and even starting to say words, sometimes with a bit of help.

How do you think reading habits in children have changed since your kids were young?

Reading habits in children have changed significantly since my own kids were young. We lived in a different era, and today's families are navigating a much more fast-paced, ever-changing societal environment with its own unique demands.

When my kids were young, screen time was hardly a concern; we didn't have to consider its potential negative effects on their social, emotional, or mental well-being. Their preference was primarily to be outdoors, engaged with friends, and participating in a sport or activity, regardless of the season. The aftermath of the pandemic, too, only added new pressures to family life.

Time is precious, and my hope is that parents, guardians, and caregivers recognize the value of being as present as they can with their young children, by creating consistent screen-free routines, establishing healthy boundaries around technology use, and continuing to foster a love for reading.

What role does imagination play in your storytelling process?

Imagination is fundamental in my storytelling process; it's simply how my mind works. I'll observe or hear something, and my thoughts spin into endless possibilities. This is precisely why it was so important for me to collaborate with people who embraced my vision. Anthony Richichi, along with my publisher Vicki Addesso Dodd, are remarkable talents who completely understood the story's direction.

A great example is the opening spread, "As an EXPLORER." The toddler character was inspired by a video of our first grandchild safely navigating through a corn maze. We watched it a couple of times, and my imagination immediately transformed the corn maze into an Amazon Jungle. That video was my ultimate inspiration.

What advice would you give to aspiring authors looking to write their first children's book?

That's a great question! I actually started toying with the idea of writing a children's book several years before Oh Little One, Who Will You Be? took shape, anticipating becoming a grandparent.

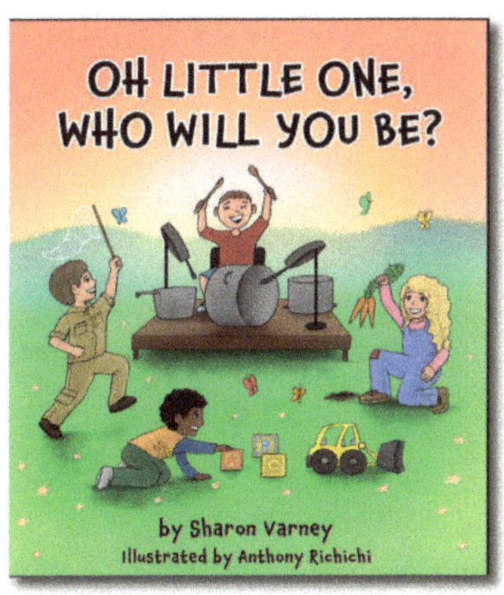

> *Oh Little One, Who Will You Be?* is a heartwarming celebration of childhood curiosity and imagination! Sharon Varney's tender storytelling, paired with Anthony Richichi's enchanting illustrations, creates a beautifully uplifting tale that inspires dreams and encourages discovery. Perfect for families seeking a timeless, magical journey through a child's eyes.

My biggest piece of advice would be to do your research and commit to continuous learning. Even with my 20+ years as an educator, I knew children's literature had its own unique style. So, I took an online course specifically on writing for children and invested in a book that guided writers on crafting stories for young readers. There are also many other valuable resources readily available online.

I've already had several aspiring authors approach me, inquiring about my journey from initial concept to final publication, and I am happy to share what I've learned.

> *Time is precious—make room for reading, connection, and wonder."*

Sharon Varney

More.
Longevity & Wellbeing
MUSHROOM
COFFEE
SUPERFOOD
BLEND
SALTED CARAMEL
VANILLA
Improves brain health, immune response, digestive function and stress relief.
Net Wt. 8.46oz (240g)
Dietary Supplement

A Journey Through Textile Embroidery And Deep Tim

Dianna Frid discusses her artistic practice, highlighting sewing, materials, and bilingualism to explore themes of language, deep time, feminine legacies, and the powerful interplay between craft and fine art.

DIANNA FRID

Weaves Time Language And Materials Into Transformative Works

As told to Noah Davis

"

Sewing text is, above all, a way to spend time with words, slowly.

Dianna Frid's work invites us into an extraordinary world where language, materials, and time converge with depth and elegance. Through her artist's books and mixed-media creations, Frid explores the tactile essence of communication, using sewing, gold, graphite, and even rocks in ways that transcend traditional notions of craft and art. Her practice challenges distinctions, embraces cultural histories, and speaks directly to our shared humanity.

Born in the vibrant textures of Mexico City and shaped by her journey to Canada and beyond, Frid has cultivated a profound understanding of how materials hold stories and meanings. Her art blends analytical thought with a palpable sensuality, uncovering the rhythms of language and the layers of deep time that shape our existence. With each stitch or inscription, she transforms the ephemeral into the enduring, reminding us of the beauty in process, material, and the echoes of forgotten histories.

In this insightful interview, Dianna Frid shares her journey—from the rhythmic sounds of her grandfather's tailor workshop to her own exploration of embroidery as a way to intertwine legibility, memory, and narrative. Frid offers a compelling perspective on the interplay between craft and fine art, the feminist legacies she draws from, and the enduring power of materials to inspire humility, wonder, and connection. Her generous and thoughtful reflections will inspire both artists and admirers alike.

Can you describe how your upbringing in Mexico and your early exposure to textiles influenced your artistic practice and the themes you explore in your work?

My maternal grandfather immigrated to Mexico City from

Rumania just before World War II. As a refugee in Mexico, he became an established women's tailor. His workshop was packed with treadle sewing machines, and his feet, and those of his staff, set the mechanism of the Singers in motion. I remember the rhythmic sounds of the sewing contraptions and the bodies gently swaying. These sways and sounds gave me a glimpse of what rhythmic processes could be, but nobody expected me to learn how to sew, and, as a result, I was not taught. Nevertheless, I gravitated to both texts and textiles on my own, particularly when I realized that all cultures have used textiles as codes. This is a lived reality in the traditional garments that people occasionally wear throughout the world. But I first noticed this in Mexico, where I was born.

You often use embroidery as a central medium. How does this choice impact the way you convey the relationships between writing, drawing, and legibility in your pieces?

Legibility and transcription inform how I work with embroidery thread—a prevalent material in my work. Spanish is my mother tongue, and English is my "stepmother language."

Dianna Frid masterfully transforms materials and ideas into profound, tactile expressions of language, history, and time, redefining boundaries of art.

Bilingualism puts me in a constant inner state of translation that influences what I choose to transcribe through sewing. Sewing text is, above all a way to spend time with words, slowly. The slowness in writing also becomes slowness in reading. This puts stress on text not just as a utilitarian method to preserve utterances, ideas and more, but as a substance that emerges and retreats, that is legible and then illegible—but not absent.

Your work seems to challenge the traditional distinctions between craft and fine art. How do you navigate the tensions and synergies between these two disciplines in your practice?

I like that you use the term synergies, and I think naming it as synergy is a way to open the conversation about affinities and not polarities. What troubles me about the typical hierarchical distinctions is that they tend to see art as communicative of new ideas and disruptive of traditions. In opposition, craft is then erroneously perceived as obedient and static. As of late, this has mercifully become of a tired notion. Sometimes establishing distinctions can be helpful to identify that a particular technique in a given culture is being passed on from one generation to another. But I taught myself how to use embroidery, and I did this because I wanted, above all, to make something other than painting. Like most people of my generation and geographical location (North America), taking art classes at a Liberal Arts university or college meant learning how to paint. And I did not want to do that, at least not all the time. So, I took refuge in sewing and found a home in art.

In what ways do you believe your work engages with feminist lineages of craft, and how do you see that relationship manifesting in your art?

This may tie into your question of traditional distinctions. I am an artist, and I am also a feminist. But I don't think in terms of being a "feminist artist" or engaged in "feminist craft". Perhaps it is more accurate to say "feminine" lineages and acknowledge that one can be any gender and tap into these. I often think of how, historically, many girls were taught how to read and write by making embroidered samplers of alphabets and piecing words together through sewing. At times this could have been another way to marginalize the feminine because sewing was an imposition, not a choice. But what would happen if we were to reintroduce this as an empowering choice for those who want to try another form of learning text?

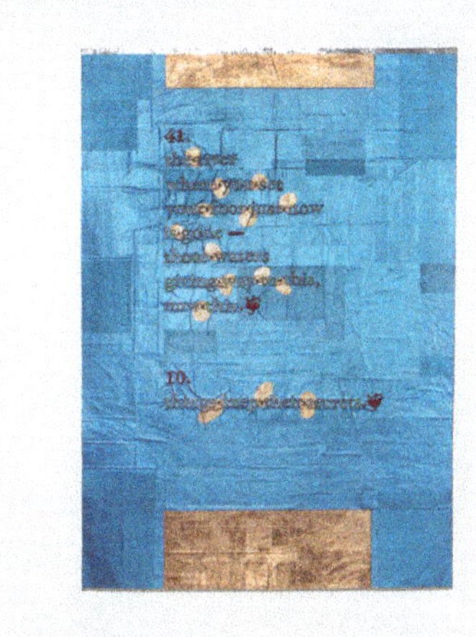

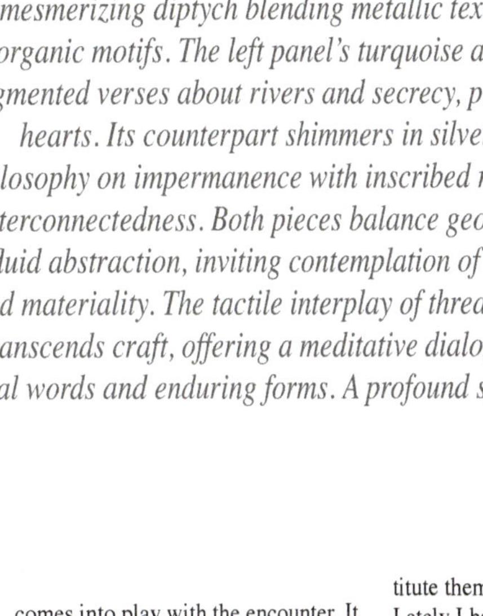

Dianna Frid's The river twice soft edges color retouched is a mesmerizing diptych blending metallic textures, poetic text, and organic motifs. The left panel's turquoise and gold layers cradle fragmented verses about rivers and secrecy, punctuated by crimson hearts. Its counterpart shimmers in silver, echoing Heraclitus' philosophy on impermanence with inscribed reflections on nature's interconnectedness. Both pieces balance geometric precision with fluid abstraction, inviting contemplation of time, transformation, and materiality. The tactile interplay of thread, leaf, and language transcends craft, offering a meditative dialogue between ephemeral words and enduring forms. A profound synthesis of touch and thought.

How do you approach the integration of sensuality and analytical thought in your work, and what significance does this duality hold for your creative expression?

There are many questions and material inclinations that drive me to make work. Yet, a good work of art, in my view, exceeds language and even context and can be felt and experienced visually—which is to say, sensually. When I look at something that moves me, most of the time I experience the resonance through the puzzle that work's facture: it is more than the sum of its constituent parts and a vessel for the concepts it carries. We could also call this resonance a "seduction" but a seduction doesn't necessarily mean that one shuts down critically when one is seduced by the sensual presence of a thing. There is a form of surrender and belief that comes into play with the encounter. It took me many years to be able to articulate with words what my work may be "about." And my ability to analyze and put this into words—for better or worse, elusively or reductively—came after a devoted process of assembling things in an attentive yet uncharted way. Once I figure out how to make something, I generally repeat the processes, because the discovery that happens through process is what leads to a series of works. And this is where analysis comes in, I think.

How do you see the role of materials in your work, particularly in terms of their historical and cultural significance, and how do they contribute to the overall narrative you aim to convey?

Language is a material. Words, letters, the curves and lines that constitute them: these are all substances. Lately I have been working with gold leaf and rocks. Gold in its purest form is nearly as old as the universe. Many rocks are thousands if not millions of years. Using these materials, alongside the slow work of sewing, points to the fact that sewing is not really that slow after all. I am not sure there is an overall narrative in my work, but these materials offer an opportunity to think about deep time and our small place in the universe. Perhaps this might contribute a measure of humility and another measure of perspective. Both are indispensable to understand that the human is only a small part of it all. And this is good.

Shaping Beauty Through Authentic Materials

"

Art never lies, it only reveals."

DIANE PIERİ

MIXED MEDIA

Diane Pieri Inspires With Her Timeless Vision And Dedication To Artistic Excellence

Diane Pieri shares her artistic journey, exploring authenticity, emotional expression, cultural influences like Indian miniatures, and her unyielding commitment to innovation, invention, and the pursuit of beauty in her work.

Diane Pieri's extraordinary artistic journey stands as a testament to creativity, perseverance, and the boundless exploration of beauty. With an illustrious career spanning over five decades, Pieri has established herself as a visionary force in the art world, merging cultural traditions, symbolic meanings, and contemporary innovations into a body of work that captivates the soul and ignites the imagination. Her mastery of delicate techniques, her fearless use of authentic materials like 23-carat gold leaf and handmade papers, and her profound ability to draw inspiration from diverse sources, such as Indian miniatures and folk art, define an artist who is unafraid to push artistic boundaries while remaining deeply rooted in truth and authenticity.

Pieri's work is more than visual art—it is an invitation into worlds of radiant color, intricate patterns, and emotional depth. Whether crafting enormous public sculptures, murals that speak to communities, or intimate pieces that reveal the inner workings of her heart and mind, Pieri imbues each creation with a sense of wonder and meaning. Her art exists at the intersection of craftsmanship and emotion, offering a glimpse into her continual pursuit of invention and beauty, as well as her unwavering devotion to sharing joy with others.

In this exclusive interview, Diane Pieri reflects on her inspirations, motivations, and the inner drive that has fueled her incredible body of work. From her early fascination with art as a young child to her profound respect for cultural storytelling and innovative techniques, Pieri shares insights into her creative process, her challenges, and her ability to continually evolve.

EDITOR'S NOTE: Diane Pieri's work is a vibrant, dynamic exploration of color, pattern, and form, embodying her signature fusion of cultural influences and contemporary innovation. The accordion-style folding artwork dazzles with bold hues—magenta, yellow, purple—and intricate motifs reminiscent of Indian miniatures and folk art, reflecting her decades-long reverence for cross-cultural storytelling. The piece's rhythmic circles and organic shapes evoke joy and movement, while its layered structure invites interaction, mirroring Pieri's belief in art as an immersive experience. Her use of authentic materials and meticulous craftsmanship shines through, reinforcing her commitment to beauty and authenticity. This work is a testament to her fearless creativity, blending tradition with playful experimentation to create a visual symphony that resonates with emotional depth and exuberance.

Prepare to be inspired by her wisdom, passion, and unrelenting commitment to offering beauty in the everyday.

How do you balance the use of symbolic meaning and abstract patterns in your work, and what role does each play in conveying your artistic message?

Every artist, over time, develops a language. What I aspire to do is have and use a language that I don't think about, like using English. I don't think about talking or formulating a sentence but, there are various times when I do search for a specific word to use, a more complex descriptive word. This is how it is making art.

Authenticity is a core principle in your art. How do the materials you choose, like 23 carat gold leaf and handmade papers, enhance the meaning of your work?

It is of utmost importance to me, as a human being, that I am authentic, in my relationships, in my word, in my actions, in my art. Art never lies, it only reveal. My art reveals who I am. This happens with everyone whether they are an artist or not. Of course children reveal all the time and are then taught to lie. I must use authentic materials because they help imbue my art with beauty, cultural integrity, sincerity, courage and strength.

Indian miniatures have deeply influenced your artistic journey. How do these influences manifest in your creations, both visually and conceptually?

I have been influenced by Indian miniatures for over 30 years now. They originally captured me because of their delicacy, their different cultural expression, their color, design and story telling. A whole world of possibilities opened up to me when I seriously started to study Indian miniatures. In fact, when I first applied for a grant to go to India, I studied with a young Indian painter so I could learn technique- how to paint a bush, a tree, grass, flowers, cloth. That first trip was thwarted by 9/11. I applied for another grant in 2012 and finally went to Northern India. What I found was completely unexpected! This was good! I discovered Indian Folk Art, which liberated me into realms of joy, dance, uncalculated vibrancy and new visual experiences. Now I have combined all the variations of this rich language- the decreet miniatures and the playful folk art.

The quote in your studio speaks to burning passion, enthusiasm, and perseverance. How do these qualities shape your creative process and the challenges you face as an artist?

I always knew I wanted to be an artist, from the age of 6 when my crayon drawing was chosen to hang in the principal's office. My parents were always very supportive throughout my educational years. However, this does not mean that I have not cried bitter tears and packed up my studio a couple of times over my long art life. As I used to tell my college students- Being an artist is a hard life, but it is a great life. I also told them that if they couldn't take rejection, they should get out then, right then.

In your pursuit to offer beauty in the everyday, what role does emotional expression play in the patterns and symbols you incorporate into your art?

Invention and beauty are what I am after. At this point in my long career, I do not differentiate between thinking and doing. This gets me into trouble. I know I am an emotional person, a feeling person, a focused person with an innate and educated understanding of color, design and all of the formal art elements. Beginning artists have a mental checklist of the formal elements and use this list to see if they have included them in their work. I do not do this anymore. For me, the important key is to kick everyone out of the studio, including myself, to paraphrase John Cage. Only then do I wander around in the space that most understands me, in search of beauty and invention.

After 25 years of artistic practice, how do you see your work evolving in the future, and what continues to inspire your exploration of new techniques or materials?

I live in fear of repeating myself! I hope I never hear anyone say that they thought they had seen the "new" work in a previous exhibition. I go on what I call "scrounging missions", after I have completed a series. This is a painful, emptiness until something unpredicted sparks my imagination. It takes patience and fortitude until something breaks through.

Exploring Migration, Belonging And Justice Through Multimedia Creations

> "
> The layering in my work reflects the complex interplay of traditions, languages, and experiences from moving across cultures."

CECILE CHONG

Cecile Chong Weaves Cultural Identity And Universal Themes In Her Multilayered Art

Cecile Chong's work blends her multicultural upbringing with universal themes of identity and belonging. Through diverse materials and mediums, her art creates dialogues around migration, history, and our interconnected humanity.

In the vibrant world of contemporary art, few voices resonate as powerfully as that of Sienna Martz. An internationally recognized sculptor and fiber artist, Sienna has carved a unique niche by intertwining traditional textile techniques with innovative material manipulation. Her commitment to sustainability shines through in every piece, as she artfully transforms plant-based, recycled, and upcycled materials into stunning works that challenge the norms of consumerism and the excesses of modern life. Each sculpture is not merely an object of beauty; it is a statement, a call to action, and a reflection of her deep-rooted ecological conscience.

Sienna's work has graced galleries and museums across the globe, from the bustling streets of New York City to the historic avenues of Rome. Her ability to engage with diverse audiences speaks to the universal themes of nature and sustainability that permeate her art. By merging aesthetic beauty with a gentle form of activism, she invites viewers to reconsider their relationship with the environment and the impact of their choices. As she continues to push the boundaries of her medium, Sienna Martz stands as a beacon of inspiration, reminding us that art can be both beautiful and transformative. In this exclusive interview with Mosaci Digest Magazine, we delve into the mind of this remarkable artist, exploring her creative process, her commitment to sustainability, and the profound messages woven into her work.

Sustainability is a key element in your work. How do you go about sourcing eco-friendly and upcycled materials for your sculptures, and how does this impact your creative process?

As an eco-conscious artist, sourcing materials is a dedicated practice in a world where most

Art & Culture

Cecile Chong's artwork masterfully blends intricate figures, foliage, and fluid watercolor backgrounds, creating a serene and nostalgic atmosphere. The delicate blue monochromatic illustrations of children and a woman evoke innocence and curiosity, harmonized with dreamy, textured washes of cream and blue hues. Overhanging leafy motifs frame the composition, enhancing its connection to nature. This piece balances timeless craftsmanship with an imaginative narrative, inviting the viewer into a tranquil, evocative moment that sparks feelings of wonder and reflection.

Cecile Chong's evocative artistry masterfully bridges cultural narratives, evoking humanity's shared essence with innovation, depth, and profound storytelling.

readily available supplies are often unsustainable. Depending on the art piece, I love sourcing secondhand clothing and fabrics at local thrift stores. Beyond that, I scour the internet searching for the most sustainable alternatives to common materials like organic kapok fiber instead of polyester stuffing, organic cotton instead of conventional cotton, and bamboo felt instead of wool felt. The plant fibers I choose to work with are incredibly high-quality which elevates my work. When working with secondhand fabrics, often the variety of woven textures and color palettes that come together while I source these supplies will help dictate how the artwork comes to life.

Your sculptures explore the adaptability of nature while critiquing unsustainable practices, especially in the textile industry. How do you balance aesthetic beauty with activism in your pieces?

I like to describe my work as a gentle form of activism. The artist in me has a primal desire to create beautiful works of art relating to nature that are both inviting and inspiring. And the activist in me has the desire to use my artistic voice as a means to encourage a more sustainable and ethical world.

Your work has been exhibited globally, from Berlin to Seoul. How do you think your sculptures resonate with audiences across different cultures, particularly in relation to environmental consciousness?

My hope is that viewers will reimagine the role of art in society, positioning my work not just as an object of beauty but as a catalyst for cultural transformation and sustainable thinking. However, since my artwork does not always visually convey concerns about climate change, animal welfare, and overconsumption viewers may not always make these connections. But because my work mimics organic and abstract forms, my work inevitably provokes thought and a kinship with the natural world regardless of the audience because we, as humans, have an innate curiosity when it comes to the natural world.

You employ both traditional textile techniques and alternative material manipulation in your sculptures. Can you describe how you merge these techniques, and what drew you to explore fiber as your primary medium?

My training in fiber arts was generally rooted in contemporary, alternative exploration rather than traditional approaches. While I learned techniques such as machine sewing and fabric dying, my mentors encouraged me to think outside of tradition and develop my own techniques of sculpting with fibers. I've always been drawn to the softness of fibers and its forgiving nature. This medium has allowed me to explore my fascination with nature through an abstract and vibrant lens.

As an artist dedicated to challenging consumerism and excess, how do you navigate the commercial art world while staying true to your ecological principles?

As an artist emerging within a digital culture, I've found utilizing commercial art forms such as social media has tremendously helped me grow my profession. I've spent years establishing my Instagram account and as a result, I have a devoted community of fellow artists and collectors who can follow and support my artistic journey. This platform has allowed me to share my ecological principles and bring more awareness to issues such as climate change, the textile waste crisis, and so on.

Your works are often described as inspired by the geometry of biology. Can you elaborate on how the natural world informs the textures, shapes, and colors in your art?

I have a deep fascination with how cells and organisms are formed through patterns and replication. I often use the transformative power of replication of a single form to create my sculptural pieces – building, layering, and structuring my work into something unexpected and quite fascinating.

Challenging Consumerism through Sculptural Beauty

Photo by Joy Masi

Sienna Martz Creates Transformative Sculptures That Merge Sustainability And Beauty

Sienna Martz uses upcycled textiles and plant-based materials to create sculptures that blend environmental activism, natural beauty, and cultural transformation, showcasing sustainability's artistic potential on a global stage.

"I like to describe my work as a gentle form of activism."

SIENNA MARTZ

Art & Culture

In the vibrant world of contemporary art, few voices resonate as powerfully as that of Sienna Martz. An internationally recognized sculptor and fiber artist, Sienna has carved a unique niche by intertwining traditional textile techniques with innovative material manipulation. Her commitment to sustainability shines through in every piece, as she artfully transforms plant-based, recycled, and upcycled materials into stunning works that challenge the norms of consumerism and the excesses of modern life. Each sculpture is not merely an object of beauty; it is a statement, a call to action, and a reflection of her deep-rooted ecological conscience.

Sienna's work has graced galleries and museums across the globe, from the bustling streets of New York City to the historic avenues of Rome. Her ability to engage with diverse audiences speaks to the universal themes of nature and sustainability that permeate her art. By merging aesthetic beauty with a gentle form of activism, she invites viewers to reconsider their relationship with the environment and the impact of their choices. As she continues to push the boundaries of her medium, Sienna Martz stands as a beacon of inspiration, reminding us that art can be both beautiful and transformative. In this exclusive interview with Mosaci Digest Magazine, we delve into the mind of this remarkable artist, exploring her creative process, her commitment to sustainability, and the profound messages woven into her work.

Sustainability is a key element in your work. How do you go about sourcing eco-friendly and upcycled materials for your sculptures, and how does this impact your creative process?

As an eco-conscious artist, sourcing materials is a dedicated practice in a world where most

Sienna Martz's innovative sculptures captivate with their biomorphic shapes and vibrant colors. Using upcycled textiles and organic textures, her works blend sustainability with artistry, evoking curiosity and connection to nature. Displayed in a minimalist gallery space, her creations challenge consumers to rethink their environmental footprint while celebrating the tactile, transformative potential of traditional and contemporary fiber art.

Sienna Martz's innovative sculptures beautifully merge nature-inspired aesthetics with ecological activism, spotlighting sustainability while redefining the artistic boundaries of fiber and alternative materials.

readily available supplies are often unsustainable. Depending on the art piece, I love sourcing secondhand clothing and fabrics at local thrift stores. Beyond that, I scour the internet searching for the most sustainable alternatives to common materials like organic kapok fiber instead of polyester stuffing, organic cotton instead of conventional cotton, and bamboo felt instead of wool felt. The plant fibers I choose to work with are incredibly high-quality which elevates my work. When working with secondhand fabrics, often the variety of woven textures and color palettes that come together while I source these supplies will help dictate how the artwork comes to life.

Your sculptures explore the adaptability of nature while critiquing unsustainable practices, especially in the textile industry. How do you balance aesthetic beauty with activism in your pieces?

I like to describe my work as a gentle form of activism. The artist in me has a primal desire to create beautiful works of art relating to nature that are both inviting and inspiring. And the activist in me has the desire to use my artistic voice as a means to encourage a more sustainable and ethical world.

Your work has been exhibited globally, from Berlin to Seoul. How do you think your sculptures resonate with audiences across different cultures, particularly in relation to environmental consciousness?

My hope is that viewers will reimagine the role of art in society, positioning my work not just as an object of beauty but as a catalyst for cultural transformation and sustainable thinking. However, since my artwork does not always visually convey concerns about climate change, animal welfare, and overconsumption viewers may not always make these connections. But because my work mimics organic and abstract forms, my work inevitably provokes thought and a kinship with the natural world regardless of the audience because we, as humans, have an innate curiosity when it comes to the natural world.

You employ both traditional textile techniques and alternative material manipulation in your sculptures. Can you describe how you merge these techniques, and what drew you to explore fiber as your primary medium?

My training in fiber arts was generally rooted in contemporary, alternative exploration rather than traditional approaches. While I learned techniques such as machine sewing and fabric dying, my mentors encouraged me to think outside of tradition and develop my own techniques of sculpting with fibers. I've always been drawn to the softness of fibers and its forgiving nature. This medium has allowed me to explore my fascination with nature through an abstract and vibrant lens.

As an artist dedicated to challenging consumerism and excess, how do you navigate the commercial art world while staying true to your ecological principles?

As an artist emerging within a digital culture, I've found utilizing commercial art forms such as social media has tremendously helped me grow my profession. I've spent years establishing my Instagram account and as a result, I have a devoted community of fellow artists and collectors who can follow and support my artistic journey. This platform has allowed me to share my ecological principles and bring more awareness to issues such as climate change, the textile waste crisis, and so on.

Your works are often described as inspired by the geometry of biology. Can you elaborate on how the natural world informs the textures, shapes, and colors in your art?

I have a deep fascination with how cells and organisms are formed through patterns and replication. I often use the transformative power of replication of a single form to create my sculptural pieces – building, layering, and structuring my work into something unexpected and quite fascinating.

Exploring Fiction And Reality Through Art

Photo by Joy Masi

Januario Jano Blurs the Boundaries Between Art, Identity, and Global Narratives

Januario Jano's interdisciplinary art examines identity, home, and cultural narratives, blending mediums to explore globalization, reality, fiction, and community engagement, while fostering cultural dialogue through initiatives like Pés Descalços and TEDxLuanda.

> "The research phase offers both a grounding foundation and a sense of openness to unexpected shifts."

JANUARIO JANO

Januario Jano is a name that resonates deeply in the contemporary art world—a multifaceted artist whose work transcends mediums and boundaries. From sculpture and video to photography, textile, sound installation, and performance, Jano's practice is a tapestry of cultural commentary, personal introspection, and social critique. With a Master's Degree in Fine Arts from Goldsmiths University in London, his work is steeped in research, allowing him to confront poignant themes like identity, home, and cultural narratives with depth and nuance. Speaking with MOsaic Digest, Jano opened up about his process, inspirations, and philosophies, offering a glimpse into the mind of an artist who not only creates but also catalyzes cultural and social transformation. Through both his art and his community initiatives, such as the Angola-based cultural collective Pés Descalços and the launch of TEDxLuanda, Jano is solidifying his position as a global artistic force, bridging past and present, fiction and reality.

The Intersection of Mediums: Building Bridges Through Art

Jano's art is a constellation of mediums, each one selected with precision to serve and enhance the ideas he seeks to communicate. His approach begins with rigorous research, a process he describes as both grounding and open to surprise. "The research phase offers both a grounding foundation and a sense of openness to unexpected shifts," he shared. "It can serve as a point of departure, facilitate and clarify the core themes or ideas I want to explore, but at the same time, it leaves room for those ideas to evolve or take new forms as I engage with the materials." By embracing a range of mediums—from tactile forms like sculpture and textile to the fluid tem-

Art & Culture

This striking installation from Januario Jano's solo exhibition, Butaiuri in Tokyo 2024, masterfully juxtaposes texture, color, and form. The central sphere showcases intricate beadwork, drawing the viewer's eye with a vivid mosaic of black, white, red, and blue. The hanging textile contrasts with its rugged, fragmented appearance, blending glossy black, fiery orange, and coarse materials. Set against a bold red backdrop, the dramatic and minimalistic setting intensifies the artwork's emotional resonance. Jano skillfully explores themes of imperfection, cultural identity, and materiality, creating a visually captivating and thought-provoking piece.

Januario Jano masterfully infuses research-driven depth into his art, creating culturally resonant, transformative works that inspire thought-provoking connections.

porality of video and sound installations—Jano creates an interplay that enriches his overall practice. "The interplay between these mediums enhances the overall depth of the work, as each medium can push the boundaries of how I communicate an idea," he explained.

Fiction, Reality, and the Stories We Tell Ourselves

At the heart of Jano's work lies a constant negotiation between fiction and reality, particularly in the context of identity and cultural narratives. For the artist, this dynamic provides both a window into contemporary issues and a framework to question deeper societal constructs. "The balance between fiction and reality in my work speaks to the complex layers of identity and cultural narratives," Jano said. "These topics challenge perceptions of what is 'true' or 'authentic' in the stories we tell or hear about ourselves and our cultures." This duality is an essential lens through which Jano approaches themes like migration, globalization, and the representation of marginalized communities. Fiction, he argues, provides a valuable space for reimagining or reframing reality, helping to address power dynamics, historic narratives, and the interconnected factors molding the global social fabric.

Art as a Response to Globalization: Collaboration and Critique

Globalization—both its opportunities and its pitfalls—is a recurring theme in Jano's art. He views the phenomenon as a crucial lens for examining the interplay of cultures, economies, and technologies, as well as a mechanism for interrogating identity. "In an increasingly interconnected world, the blending of cultures, economies, and technologies creates new spaces for dialogue but also raises questions of power, ownership, and identity," he reflected. Through his work, Jano creates spaces where histories and narratives collide, allowing abstract ideas—like the cultural flows brought on by globalization—to gain tangible, physical form. This critique of globalization is not merely an artistic exercise but a call for reflection. "Art becomes a platform to reflect on how globalization reshapes our understanding of self and other, exposing the ways identities are constructed, deconstructed, and recontextualized in this global context," he explained.

Cultural Leadership and the Role of the Artist

Beyond his own practice, Jano is deeply invested in cultural development and social transformation. His initiatives, such as Pés Descalços and TEDxLuanda, exemplify his belief that art and cultural innovation should have a broad, tangible impact on communities. "Pés Descalços started as I felt the need to engage and contribute to the local cultural and artistic landscape outside my own practice," Jano said. "These cultural initiatives are parallel to my artistic practice in fostering community, dialogue, and engagement with cultural narratives." Rather than viewing his artistic practice and community initiatives as separate entities, Jano integrates them, embodying a philosophy that art should have both personal and public resonance. "I see the artist as both a creator and a facilitator, someone who bridges diverse perspectives, encouraging collective reflection, social development, and critical thinking," he affirmed.

Decoding Identity Through Research and the Material World

Jano's art is deeply informed by research—a key element that underpins every step of his creative process. His studious approach allows him to excavate layers of meaning, uncovering connections between themes like identity, home, and cultural memory. "When dealing with themes like identity and home, the research might involve delving into historical narratives, personal stories, cultural identity, and production," Jano explained. The resulting work is a harmony of the conceptual and the material, with mediums chosen to amplify the project's core themes. For instance, Jano might explore the concept of "home" through the architectural, emotional, and cultural dimensions of space, while a study of identity might draw on post-colonial theory, displacement, or oral histories. "These multidisciplinary approaches offer a rich context that informs the final decisions of the project in hand," he said.

The Body as a Canvas of Culture and History

The body is a recurring symbol within Jano's practice, representing the nexus of space, culture, and history. As both a physical and metaphorical vessel, the body becomes a site where these complex themes come alive. "The body in my work plays a pivotal role—it acts as a symbol, representing the intersection of space, culture, and history," Jano shared. His projects explore how the body carries both memory and meaning, functioning as a site of negotiation and contestation within broader societal frameworks. Jano's depiction of the body varies across projects. In some cases, it appears through physicality, as in his sculptures or performances, while in others, its absence or fragmentation is evoked through video, photography, or sound installations. The flexibility in these representations underscores Jano's ability to adapt his artistic language to match the nuances of each project's message.

Looking Forward: A Path of Connection and Transformation

Januario Jano is redefining what it means to be an artist in a globalized world. His ability to weave research, storytelling, and a diverse range of materials into a cohesive artistic vision transforms his work into more than just a visual experience—it becomes a powerful commentary on identity, cultural evolution, and the forces shaping our shared future. Through his artistic practice and his roles as a cultural leader, Jano has made it clear that art is not just about aesthetics but also about building bridges, challenging norms, and fostering transformation. As he continues to innovate and explore, his work serves as a compelling reminder of art's potential to illuminate the complexities of the human condition in an ever-connected world.

BENZINGA

And so much more ...

Key Partnerships and Future Initiatives

Expanding the Boundaries of Literature.

Being featured in Novelist Post means gaining visibility not just in print edition, but across the entire media spectrum in the US, UK, Europe and beyond

Key Media Partnerships:

- Associated Press (reaching 50%+ of global population)
- Benzinga (5M monthly visitors)
- Nexstar (68% U.S. TV household penetration)
- Major search engines: Google News, Google, Yahoo, Bing, Ask
- EIN Press Wire coverage
- NewYox Media magazines coverage (Mosaic Digest, Reader's House, CEO Vision, Beauty Prime...)

Broadcast & Digital Coverage:

- Major U.S. network affiliates
- 150+ million monthly radio website users
- 500+ UK media outlets
- Minimum 5 to 20 media placements per country (Albania to Zambia)
- Enhanced SEO positioning with quality backlinks from each media
- Optimized presence on e-commerce platforms)
- Featured across 4000+ media platforms in the US, UK, Europe and beyond

Distribution Highlights:

- Accessible online, through social media, digital (flip), and print formats.
- The print edition is available permanently in over 190 countries.
- Distributed by major retailers such as Amazon, Barnes & Noble, Walmart, Blackwells, Fishpond, Abebooks, and Waterstones.
- Also available through local retailers, spanning from Alaska to Wisconsin in the United States.
- Print edition available for a lifetime.

contact us today for an interview opportunity at
editor@novelistpost.com

Available in
PRINT

Americas to Australia Europe to Africa Reader's House is available over 190 countries and thousands of retaiers, platforms including Amazon, Barnes & Noble, Walmart, Waterstone's .....

ELECTRONIC

It is an electronic (flip book) format and interactive. Accessable from electronic devices like pc, smart phone, notepads..

ONLINE

All interviews, we conduct make them accessable online for free.

SOCIAL MEDIA

We are on Facebook, Instagram and X. Please follow us on social media @novelistpost

contact us today for an interview opportunity at
editor@novelistpost.com

Save up to 50% when you order 10 or more from the same issue

Subscribe Now!

YES! I would like a subscription to

☐ Current Issue for

☐ One-Year Subscription (_____ Issues) for

☐ Two-Year Subscription (_____ Issues) for

☐ I am a renewing a current subscription ☐ I am a new subscriber

Name: ______________________ Phone: ______________

Shipping Address: ______________________

Billing Address: ______________________

Email: ______________________

☐ Yes, I would like to receive updates, newsletters and special offers

☐ No, I would NOT like to receive updates, newsletters and special offers

Payment Type: ☐ Check ☐ Bank transfer ☐ Wise ☐ PayPal

____

____

Please mail this form to:

Magazine Name:

www.ingramcontent.com/pod-product-compliance
Lightning Source LLC
Chambersburg PA
CBHW041206100726
47911CB00016B/872